Close to Paradise

The Gardens of Naples, Capri
and the Amalfi Coast

Robert I. C. Fisher

Close to Paradise

*The Gardens of Naples, Capri
and the Amalfi Coast*

F

FRANCES LINCOLN LIMITED
PUBLISHERS

To my mother,
whose abiding love,
grace, faith and
understanding have been
my most trustworthy
compass points,
and to the 'father' of this book,
Baron Massimo Ricciardi

Frances Lincoln Limited
4 Torriano Mews
Torriano Avenue
London NW5 2RZ
www.franceslincoln.com

Page 1: A view of Lord Astor's
Villa Tritone, Sorrento.
Pages 2: Sir Lawrence
Alma-Tadema's *Juno* adorns
the Villa Tritone's bay parapet.
Right: The Window of the Siren
at the Villa Tritone, Sorrento.

Contents

Introduction
The Most Beautiful Place in the World?

Not all of Paradise was lost. A luxuriant dollop of it – Campania – lingers on in southern Italy. This sun-blest region, which includes Naples, Capri, Sorrento and the Amalfi Coast, is like no other place on earth. With powers of attachment which recall those of that Lotus land which cast a spell over the sailors of Odysseus, Campania exerts a pull on travellers as inexorable as that of the moon upon the tides. Over the centuries, many an artist, emperor and poet has paid homage to its landscape, and the fabled signs of nature's grandstanding they witnessed are still there for us to wonder at today: silently ticking Mount Vesuvius, the spellbindingly seductive Blue Grotto and the beauteous Bay of Naples. If much of Campania's countryside remains Homeric in its rough-hewn power, the past two centuries have seen the development of an array of grace notes – idyllic gardens, palatial villas, picturesque villages – that have largely de-fanged the area's primordial terrain.

In fact, Campania's wide array of gardens has transformed it into a kind of Eden. As with any Eden, there is seduction, but in this case, it is horticultural, thanks to estates of such splendour that they are almost too beautiful to be real. When visiting them, while writing this book, often I would tour a garden and speak to fellow visitors who felt that they had just died and gone to heaven. In fact, there was one gentleman who did not even believe there was such a place, but after seeing the Villa Cimbrone he changed his mind.

It was in this part of the ancient world that Homer believed the three Sirens sang their haunting song to try to entrap Odysseus and his sailors. The wily navigator, however, managed to outwit them by having himself tied to the ship's mast and sealing his crew's ears with wax. The legend of these Sirens is still reflected in the name of the ancient Roman town called Surrentum, the 'Land of the Sirens'. Today, considering the bewitching spell the resort town of Sorrento has cast ever since, one must wonder if the name really means Surrender. For century after century, travellers – Virgil, Emma Hamilton, Richard Wagner, Vita Sackville-West, Lord William Waldorf Astor and Greta Garbo among them – have done precisely that. These days, visitors still hum the sweet ritornello 'Come Back to Sorrento', unable to get the song or the region out of their heads.

Edenic beauty is its own reward, but Campania enlarges the process with the contribution of people with seemingly unlimited knowledge, skill and taste. And the fact that this paradise has been hallowed by so many historic figures makes one realize that the spirit of these gardens is not just in their style and beauty but also in their individual stories, many of which go way back, embracing ideas and innovation, social and economic history, biography, the interaction of cultures, world history and so much else. The gardens, in other words, are not just gardens: ultimately, each garden is what it is what it is, like Gertrude Stein's rose, but behind the physical splendours and visual delights lie the inner workings that are at the heart of every historic garden, and these are what I have tried to focus on here.

Welcome to Campania Felix

With golden lemon trees and the blaze of bougainvilleas, its soft breezes, emerald grottoes, mesmerizing vistas and an array of awe-strikingly beautiful villas, Campania has long been known for its general gorgeousness. Erstwhile pleasure dome to the Roman emperors, who called it Campania Felix, 'the happy land', this province has been straining the vocabulary of visitors from the time when the Sirens tried to lure Odysseus into their lair near Sorrento. Ever since, it has been difficult for steersmen from any land to pass by this part of southern Italy, which stretches south from the Bay of Naples and the Sorrentine peninsula to the Amalfi coast and the Bay of Salerno, all rimmed by the true-bluest waters of the Mediterranean. Unlike Homer's hero, today's travellers willingly submit to the region's sights and pleasures.

The gateway to the region is the city of Naples, the supreme character metropolis of Italy, whose virtues are unsurpassed: an idyllic location on the Bay of Naples, a storied past, monumental architectural treasures and an exuberant mode of life. Near by, in the bay, are the isles of Capri and Ischia, bequests of some distant volcanic eruption that compensated for the destruction it wrought with the gift of spectacular scenery.

Campania's genteelly faded Belle-Epoque history is best exemplified by the city of Sorrento, whose palatial hotels rose seemingly overnight in the late 1890s to accommodate the influx of lords and ladies attracted to the spot. Further to the south is the Amalfi coast, perhaps the most divine 30-mile/48-kilometre stretch of water, land and habitation on the continent, or anywhere. Here, the visitor will find Positano, famed as the most photographed fishing village in the world; Amalfi, prime jewel in the region's medieval crown; and, situated halfway to heaven on the flanks of Monte Cerreto, the town of Ravello, whose Villa Rufolo once captivated Richard Wagner and Greta Garbo.

Guidebooks reveal a wide array of attractions and sights in Campania but, despite its wealth of palatial villas, historic churches and charming villages, it is first and foremost a playground. After all, it was the Neapolitans who coined the maxim *dolce far niente* – 'It is sweet to do nothing.' As they have done from the days of the ancient Romans onwards, travellers head here to master the art of doing just that – nothing – and do it very well. Celebrated personages, including emperors and kings, have come and continue to come to partake of innocent delights – sunning, sailing, fishing, wining, dining, relaxing. Serious artists come to work – Wagner's *Parsifal*, Ibsen's *Doll's House* and works by Virginia Woolf, Graham Greene and Tennessee Williams came to life here – while Romance will always have its way: pairs who frolicked on the scene include Nelson and Lady Hamilton, and Elizabeth Taylor and Richard Burton.

And in such a naturally fertile region, it should not surprise the reader to learn that the list of pleasure activities included gardening. The salubrious combination of sun with other essential elements, such as the soil, with which nature blessed southern Italy makes Campania a gardener's dream. Over the course of several millennia, the area's potential lured a steady flow of conquering civilizations who invaded Italy, including Greek adventurers, Roman senators, the Moors and the French. Of all these visiting nations, it was the English who succumbed most thoroughly to Campania's power of seduction. Over the nineteenth and twentieth centuries, a small army of English aristocrats made Campania into personal fiefdoms, transforming villas and gardens into mini-worlds of elegance, privilege, comfort and beauty.

A Garden in Search of a View

The verdant growth seen today did not come about lickety-split, however. Far from it. Embedded with countless rocks and a mountainous terrain, Campania was not a natural Eden. From the beginning, cultivation of the land involved an uphill fight – literally. As Astolphe de Custine remarked in his *Mémoires et voyages* (1830), 'In this incomprehensible landscape only the sea is horizontal, while that of terra firma is nearly perpendicular.' Not only plantings but also human settlements had nowhere else to go but up, with results like the cliff of cottages that today crowd the hillsides overlooking Positano and make the view of its harbour such a picturesque sight. Fortunately, nature came to the early plantsmen's rescue with a bounty of mountains – Vesuvius to the north and the Lattaris to the south – that provided enough protection from the harsh winds and scorching temperatures to make the thought of gardening a possibility. Even so, those bent on planting had to do so in the narrow plots of land, called *chiazze*, which were often carved out of the hillsides.

Clearly, to make peace with obstinacy of such magnitude required masses of creativity. And to elevate simple plantings into horticultural extravaganzas required ingenuity too, plus a bent for civil engineering. These qualities eventually led to the development of terraced landscaping, wherein plantings were made in a series of descending levels, like steps carved to conform to and more or less hide the unworkable natural slope of the land. This type of garden was referred to as a *giardino pensile*, or hanging garden; in this sense the gardens of Campania are often truly Babylonic. (Today, the term often refers to rooftop versions.) In situations where the setting opened on to a lovely vista, the design of the stepped area was often elaborated through the addition of artistic *terrazzamenti*, belvederes and pergolas, and the siting of viewing points, to enhance the gardens' sea-gazing potential.

The step-design gardens offered *volo d'uccello* (bird's-eye views) over a terrain that was full of views. In Ravello, to name one instance, a stroll through the sea-facing stepped beds of the Villa Rufolo, set 1,400 feet/426 metres above the Bay of Salerno, makes you feel as if your own weight is irrelevant. From the Belvedere of Infinity of the nearby Villa Cimbrone, the blue of the sky can imperceptibly blend with the blue of the ocean, creating the illusion of a horizonless world. Visit the Villa San Michele garden on the Siren Heights of Capri, which perhaps claims the loftiest perch of them all, and you may be as close to heaven as you will ever get.

Although these gardens offer some of the most breathtaking views this side of a NASA space capsule, they do so not just for reasons of spectacle. During the Middle Ages, the devastation wrought by Saracen pirate invasions sent Campania's native populations fleeing to the hills, where they built eagle's-nest-high towns and villages – Ravello and Anacapri, to name two – which offered protection from the invaders. With the onset of more peaceful times the local *costieri* were happy to move down to the slopes at the water's edge, as at Positano, where streets and passageways take the form of *scalinatelli* (staircases), and whitewashed houses – of necessity built on top of one another – create the appearance of miniature kasbahs or Cycladic villages: the area's archetypal *casa mediterranea* style developed when Campania was part of ancient Magna Grecia. During the relatively peaceful eighteenth and nineteenth centuries, houses were often 'enlarged' through the addition of terraces and extensive balconies, designed to take advantage of incomparable *vista del mare*; the value of a house along the Amalfi coast is still dependent on how many of its windows face the sea.

Down History's Garden Path

The first of the cultures to nurture Campania's gifts of the earth were the Greeks, who founded Neapolis (Naples) as early as the fourth century BC. However, Campania's real efflorescence – culturally and horticulturally – had to wait until the first century BC for the ancient Caesars to discover that the seaside air was a cure for Rome's stifling heat. Soon, elaborate pleasure palaces with landscaped grounds dotted the shoreline of the Bay of Naples. Near here, on Capri, Tiberius created the Villa Jovis, a huge palace whose terraced gardens historians have compared to the so-called hanging gardens of ancient Babylon. At Baia, across the bay, Nero ordered that his imperial estate be embellished with sumptuous gardens, and then added a few vineyards. At the same time, a thriving resort crowd was transforming Pompeii and Herculaneum into their own Côte d'Azur, a fantasyland of lavish villas and atrium-gardens whose plantings bloomed with all the splendour and alacrity of Jack's magical beanstalk. This was, of course, before the citizenry could even think of regretting being downwind from Vesuvius, the volcanic giant whose mineral enrichments were the source of their gardens' fertility, but whose eruption would one day cause their tragic entombment.

Between the fall of Rome in the fourth century BC and the onset of the Middle Ages, European interest in gardening gradually lost momentum. Crowding the world stage were a host of other preoccupations, the most dire being the much-feared plague, followed closely by baronial wars and other distractions. Perhaps reflecting a need for refuge from these, the *Hortus conclusus* (the contained or enclosed garden) became popular in medieval times, especially but not only in cloisters of religious buildings such as monasteries. The gardens of the medieval *chiostro del paradiso* (cloisters of paradise) of Amalfi and Sorrento are examples.

The architecture of such cloisters reflected influences from both the Norman and Arab cultures. The latter had been introduced into the area centuries earlier through the colonization of Sicily by Moors on their eastward march. In the eleventh century Sicily had fallen under Norman domination, and in the following century Norman mercenaries extended their rule over the southern half of Italy, wresting control of Naples from the Lombards. After the eleventh-century defeat of the Hohenstaufen kings of Sicily, Naples and the kingdom of Sicily were given by Pope Clement IV to Charles of Anjou, who moved the capital from Palermo to Naples and made it into an Angevin showplace. In the wake of the Normans, artistic influence came to Campania from the north, seen in Naples's grand Angevin Gothic churches; and from Sicily in Moorish-style Arab–Norman architecture). This union of styles allowed the cross and crescent to live side by side and, among other things, introduced new horticultural values. Suddenly, gardens had convoluted Moorish designs, ornamented with flowers bedded out in Middle Eastern carpet patterns, watercourse motifs, and exotic flowers and fruits newly imported from Sicily and the Middle East: iris and jasmine, lemons and mandarin oranges, tangerines and apricots.

During the fourteenth century the arts blossomed once again, as Naples welcomed Boccaccio, Giotto and Petrarch. The newly wealthy flaunted their buying power by glorifying their gardens with expanded terraces planted with masses of fragrant flowers, allowed to grow without restraint. The simplicity of medieval gardens was abandoned for lush, romantic *paradisi*, best seen in Ravello's Villa Rufolo, an Arab–Norman extravaganza right out of *A Thousand and One Nights*. This Saracenic style added a flash of flamboyance, a flame of fantasy. Minimalism was out; exuberance was the new order. By the fifteenth century, political turmoil had subsided, allowing the development of increased avenues of trade between Italy and the Middle East, which in turn led to increased wealth among the local population.

While the Renaissance took root in Naples – in 1490, Alfonso II commissioned the Florentine architect Giuliano da Maiano to create a suburban villa, the Poggio Reale, outside Naples, and added a terraced garden to the city's Castel Nuovo – it quickly made room for the styles of the sixteenth century. A taste for the picturesque and exotic code of manners was accelerated by one of Sorrento's own, namely Torquato Tasso, author of the 1575 poem 'Jerusalem Delivered', a homage to the First Crusade wherein the hero conquers the holy city. Tasso's garden ideal was one of earthly delights, quivering with romantic implications and seductive possibilities. The most talked-about section in his best-selling epic – describing the seduction of a Christian knight, Rinaldo, by the 'infidel' sorceress

The Upper Terrace of the Villa Rufolo was extensively restored by Sir Francis Neville Reid in the nineteenth century.

Armida – takes place in such a garden setting. Though he did not specify it by name, Tasso may have been familiar with the existence of the gardens of Villa Rufolo, in Ravello, even then widely celebrated as an iconic setting for romance. Thanks to Tasso, gardens were henceforth empowered to play a character role in drama, as they had so often done on the pastoral stage.

In 1738, Charles III de Bourbon established Naples as the capital of the Kingdom of the Two Sicilies. Charles and later his son, Ferdinand IV, commanded that the regalia of royalty bedeck the entire kingdom, including even the crown's grounds and gardens. The Reggia di Caserta – a palace meant to outrival the Palace of Versailles in France – was chosen as the premier model for the latest upticks in garden design: floral parterres, allées without end, symmetrical plantings and fountains overlaid with sculptural ornamentation. The gardens at the royal palaces at Capodimonte and Portici were similarly embellished at the same time. With this symbolic wave of its imperial hand, the Bourbon dynasty established a new standard of garden fitness, effectually restricting nature's capricious waywardness. This was reaffirmed after the French incursion of 1806, when Napoleon's brother Jerome Bonaparte founded, in 1807, Naples's mammoth botanical garden, the Orto Botanico, to order and categorize the plant species of the region.

But once again, floral frivolity had dared to raise its pretty head, this time in the form of a charming 'English Garden' discreetly hidden within the park at Caserta. This was the brainchild of Sir William Hamilton, English emissary to the Neapolitan court and later husband of the daring Emma, whose flame had attracted Nelson's inner moth. At the same time the grounds of the vast royal palace atop the Capodimonte hill (overlooking Naples), along with Ferdinand I's Villa La Floridiana (perched on the city's Vomero hill) – both designed by Federico Degenhardt – were being transformed into English-style 'parks'. This proved to be the prelude to an invasion – a benign one, for a change – by a fleet of plant-loving Englishmen.

Milordi Inglesi: The English Arrive

Along with Sir William, significant numbers of other English gentlefolk had arrived in Italy, drawn initially by sympathy with Italy's efforts to resist Napoleon's claims of domination. By the time

Adorned with its famous majolica benches, the Grand Terrace of Il San Pietro overlooks the sea and, in the distance, Positano.

that conflict had been resolved, in Italy's favour, many of the visiting British, in thrall to the charms of southern Italy, had elected to stay on for a while. Little by little, the while became extended by years, and then lifetimes. Over the course of the nineteenth and twentieth centuries, the sun-dazed expatriates built for themselves grand houses, which then required equally grand gardens.

Only some god-like being could have done more to beautify Campania than did the English, so grateful were they for its gifts of blue skies, balmy breezes and unlimited sunshine, especially when contrasted with the cold and frigid 'civilized' Kent-and-Surrey comforts of back home. Of course, in their hopes of finding a climatic Nirvana, they had been in the habit of dashing off to foreign lands at the drop of a top hat, secretly nurturing the dream of a private Garden of Eden, a place where eternal sunshine and a placid sea would embrace them every day of the year, where strange flowers thrived in rocky crevices; ripe fruit dangled for the plucking; wine was plentiful and cost only a few pence; and apparel was free of tight lacings and bony stays. Time would be of no account, rather than of the essence.

This is the dream these would-be Adams and Eves sought ,beginning in the eighteenth century when many shivering Englishmen and women were explosively energized by travel bulletins from Italy. Captivated by the tales of Sir William Hamilton, the watercolours of J.M.W. Turner and 'Giovanni Ruskino', and first-hand accounts by such influential tastemakers as George Howard – of the eponymous castle – and Georgiana, Duchess of Devonshire, English *gran turisti* began to heed the siren call of the Mediterranean muse.

At the head of this cavalcade was *il turismo d'elite*. J.M.W. Turner, the landscape artist, arrived in 1819, John Ruskin in 1841. Lady Blessington, whose visit to Naples in 1823 produced one of the first published reports about the area, *The Idler in Italy*, wrote that visitors to Amalfi were 'like angel visits, few and far between', implying that travel activity from the homeland was as yet feeble. But a symbolic clash of cymbals occurred on 12 January 1853, with the opening of the Vietri–Amalfi road, today known as the Amalfi Drive, which led to the birth of a new industry: Tourism, with a capital T. No longer viewed as a string of fishing villages and decrepit fortresses, Campania became a must-do destination for pleasure- and holiday-seekers. The credit for jumpstarting its transformation belonged to the English.

The rewards of gardening were already well known to the voluntary expats; now, inspired afresh by their new environment, they set to gardening à la Italienne, *con gusto*. Reporting from her perch at the Villa Gallo, at Capodimonte, Lady Blessington described the miracle: 'Many of the plants, to be found only in hothouses with us, here grow luxuriantly in the open air . . . terraces rise over terraces, filled with flowering shrubs, and giving a notion of the Hanging Gardens of Babylon.' By the early twentieth century, Lord William Waldorf Astor had discovered that the streets of Sorrento were paved not with gold but with a far better thing: sunshine. Before long, many of his English brethren had put down roots in the form of permanent abodes, surrounded by grounds tended by skilled nurserymen. Transformed by the idyll rich, Campania took on the raiment of a millionaire's pleasance, as their gardens, described in this book, prove: Sir William Hamilton's 'English' garden at Caserta, Francis Neville Reid's Villa Rufolo in Ravello, Lord William Waldorf Astor's Villa Tritone in Sorrento, Lord Grimthorpe's Villa Cimbrone in Ravello and Sir William Walton's La Mortella on Ischia. The statued and stately garden terraces of England's grand estates (which dot so many pages of Disraeli's novels) were left behind, happily replaced by a new picturesque vision of gardening.

Paradise of the Picturesque

If nineteenth-century Romantics had been searching for the ultimate scenographic landscape, they needed look no further than Campania. The geography might have been the work of stagecraft, rather than nature. An array of 'Gothic' features – stormy crags and steep precipices, dark valleys and strange grottoes, everything but a signpost reading 'Hermits and pilgrims welcome' – spoke directly to the Romantic ideal. Adding a picturesque layer to the scene were traces left by other cultures – Byzantine, Arab, Norman, Saracen, Gothic – including, according to Lady Blessington, 'dilapidated castles, watch-towers, churches, and convents so admirably placed as to appear as if erected as ornaments in the enchanting landscape'.

Landscape painters loved every bit of it. A precedent of sorts had been set in the seventeenth century with the scenes of Campania painted by Salvator Rosa, whose paintings of a bandit-ridden countryside of haunted caves and towering cliffs had caught the imagination of Europe. But although discovery by outsiders of the most dazzling setpieces – the Amalfi coast, Capri and Sorrento – coincided with the age of the Grand Tour, it was not until later in the nineteenth century that artists, easels and paintboxes in tow, became a felt presence. Among the European painters who produced memorable landscape paintings at the time were Leo von Klenze, Thomas Ender, Oswald Achenbach and several Scuola di Posillipo notables, including Teodoro Duclere and Theodor Witting. For the rich, fashionable and highly cultivated of the era, these *vedute* had the come-hither effect that postcards would later exert on twentieth-century tourists.

Transformed into a place of the imagination by poem and painting, Campania and its sleeping-beauty towns like Ravello and Sorrento – recently awakened by arriving English – were hailed as Romanesque Edens. Rejecting the present for the glamour of the chivalric past, neo-medievalists rejoiced in the once-upon-a-time atmosphere of the Amalfi coast; a large part of the appeal of the 'antiquely picturesque' was its *tempus fugit* associations with age and decay, and for signs of these, the Amalfi coast's medieval relics could not be improved upon. Its 'Middle Ages' vibe found a perfect response in the Picturesque movement, which, back home in England, had been growing ever more fashionable and now found expression in the gardens and villas of Campania.

The Sirens Are Still Singing

Today the siren song not only continues to tempt Wall Streeters, Main Streeters, deadline beaters and many others, but delivers completely. For each new observer of the scene, Campania comes to life like an Old Master painting: the blue sea, the fishing boats, a celestial sky, inviting sands, eternal sunshine and ravishing gardens.

This book journeys through valleys, over cliffs and across bridges in search of Campania's most ravishing gardens. It finds, in most cases, not plantsmen but 'artists': exceptional gardeners who created Campania at its cornucopia-ed best. It is almost impossible to reduce these gorgeous patches of earth to mere words on paper. The most gifted writer's voice must be silenced before these gardens' multiple splendours: the sumptuous settings, the artistic architecture and tasteful ambience. But these qualities cannot so easily elude the camera's eye. Since a single image can speak volumes, you will, I hope, find in the photographs what my words cannot express. I take my cue from that wonderful welcome so many Italians extend to a newly arrived traveller: '*Le faccio vedere*' – 'Let me show you.'

A rare standard rose draws all eyes in the courtyard garden of the Palazzo Murat, Positano.

I

NAPOLI NOBILISSIMA

Naples and Environs

Sun Souci

Villa d'Avalos

Posillipo

It is hard not to like a district called 'the place where all unhappiness ends'. Today called Posillipo, this scenic promontory just west of Naples was baptized by the city's first settlers, the ancient Greeks, who called it Pausilypon, a 'pause from pain' – a nickname prompted by its superlatively fertile soil, seductive bayside setting and paradisical climate. In the age of the emperors, Pausilypon became a favoured retreat of the powerful and privileged who, while here, were able to shed the onerous duties of greatness in exchange for luxury and carefree indolence. The Caesars, *sans souci*, forgot their woes here and Virgil, Rome's greatest poet, chose this area as his favoured home. In Rome he may have sung of 'arms and the man' but here his muse inspired him to recreate the magnificent scenery in his *Georgics*, the very first pastoral poem. While the upper middle class colonized Pompeii and Herculaneum on the other side of the Bay of Naples, Pausilypon was the enchanted coign that emperors and poets called their own.

Today there are some fortunate Neapolitans who have followed in their wake. Although large stretches of Posillipo now resemble Naples's congested city centre, the coastline of the suburb is still studded with romantic villas – their styles ranging from neo-classic to neo-Gothic to neo-Egyptian – largely constructed in the late nineteenth century. Inevitably, a goodly number now adjoin apartment houses, but a few have survived with their estates intact, though, sadly, even fewer with the gardens that once made the district synonymous with beauty. Standing out among these few, for pure horticultural deliciousness, is the Villa d'Avalos, the domain of Principessa Maria d'Avalos.

Sheltered by towering Aleppo pines, the villa's garden unfolds in a series of grand terraces linked by stone steps – to enable navigation of the steep hillside – and dotted with belvederes opening on to

A beautiful view of the Bay of Naples as seen from the lower terrace of the Villa d'Avalos.

striking panoramas of the Bay of Naples, with Mount Vesuvius, that most celebrated of volcanoes, dead centre across the water. 'When it looks close enough to touch, it foretells rain; when it appears far away, we plan a picnic,' the principessa says.

As she guides a guest around the garden – a motorized go-cart parked nearby 'has more miles on it than my car' – she notes, with just a hint of pride, that hers is the only Posillipo garden with its original garden paths; nearly all the other estates have added roads, 'to accommodate Fiats'. One of these paths, a twisty stone one, hedged by caper-bearing shrubs and shaded by Canary Island pines (*Pinus canariensis*), leads to the garden's main terrace, whose stonework is softened by bursts of pink and orange hibiscus surrounding a papyrus pool. Stone benches and a suite of wrought-iron table and chairs allow this terrace to serve as a living room, though the spacious neo-classical house is only a few feet away. The terrace was the creation of Herta von Siemens, daughter of the founder of the industrial firm of that name and owner of the estate in the late nineteenth century. She also adorned the main house, initially constructed in

Opposite: A walkway lined with bougainvillea and geraniums leads to the main house, shaded by a spiky-leaved bunya-bunya tree (*Araucaria bidwillii*) seen on the right. Above: The back terrace is decorated with a floor of Vietri tiles; in the foreground is a Romanesque capital used as a planter for an hibiscus.

1871, with a grand colonnade, the finishing touch to a renovation begun by Etienne-Jules Marey, a scientist noted for his research into locomotion (the photographer Eadweard Muybridge often used the laboratory Marey built on the property).

In 1936, the villa was bought by Prince Carlo d'Avalos, who often entertained musical greats here (today, his son Francesco d'Avalos is one of Italy's most noted composers). Since 1972, the house has belonged to Maria and her late husband, Domenico Viggiani, who wrote much of his landmark book *I tempi di Posillipo* (Electa, 1989) here. Now in her eighth decade, Principessa Maria is testimony to the value of getting out there every day and gardening. While she

now delegates most of the donkeywork to a young man, she still loves to 'wake up every morning and go out and fight with the day'.

While Posillipo is famed for its fertility – the villas here were once all self-sustaining, thanks to their own farms – its tufaceous cliffs overlooking the bay do not provide good soil and the principessa has to resort to starting many of her flowers in pots. '*Nothing* is easy to grow,' she notes, 'but succulents and cacti are less of a struggle.' The summer sun, too, poses its own challenges: from June to September rain is rare, and so she has to water her plants often during this period. 'Happily, even on diabolically sunny days, there are cool breezes from the bay. In fact, I rarely cut down the trees because the wind can be your garden's enemy.'

The principessa firmly believes in letting nature have its way. If, for instance, an Aleppo pine (*Pinus halepensis*) begins to grow over the path of an outlook, she will allow it to continue doing so. 'In Italian gardens, you cannot demand perfectionism. You have to like nature the way she is. That is what lends our gardens so much charm, compared, say, to the French and German styles.' Charming, indeed, is the main garden path, which meanders from a high belvedere to a

Above: A sole oleander lends a touch of red to the blue-on-blue vista.
Right: Lovely pathways link the descending levels of the garden, including this one shaded by swamp paperbark trees and umbrella pines. The balustrade is adorned with carved pine cones, stone urns (topped by pink crassula) and stone planters cascading with mesembryanthemums, succulents from South Africa.

staircase-accessed pergola some feet below to a stand of pines to yet another belvedere. If alone, you can feel as though you are enclosed in a landscape painting from the Scuola di Posillipo – a school of nineteenth-century landscape painting that counted Antoon van Pitloo, Gonsalvo Carelli and Giacinto Giagante among its members – which immortalized on canvas the locale's many picturesque coves and hills. The sensation deepens when you turn westwards, where the view encompasses a parapet crowned with imposing terracotta urns that frame a vista over the Tramontana cove. Looking eastwards over the garden brings into view a neo-Gothic castle, a massive structure built in the late nineteenth century by the Princes d'Abro, whose estate adjoined the villa's grounds.

In almost *pied-à-mer* fashion, the lowest terrace of the Villa d'Avalos is set just above the bay. Adorned with chairs, settees and tables, it beautifully accommodates guests who assemble here to admire the view. This particular spot has cast its spell on holidaymakers for centuries. Make that millennia, for the terrace is set with remarkable ancient Roman ruins that scholars date to the age of Augustus. At that time, Posillipo mostly comprised the villa of Vedio Pollio, a millionaire freedman whose riches and excess were so notorious that they were immortalized in the comical figure of Trimalchio in Petronius's *Satyricon*.

Vedio Pollio had other claims to notoriety, notably the charge that he liked to fatten his moray eels on the flesh of his slaves. Whether or not that is true, from the bayside terrace at the Villa d'Avalos you can spot the stone outlines of ancient *aquaria* – holding pens for farmed fish – just below the waves. In fact, the bay has risen in recent centuries and now floods an entire floor of Roman rooms (located beneath the lowermost terrace, with one still visible and covered with magnificent frescoes in the 2nd Pompeiian Style).

History tells us that in 15 BC, Vedio Pollio prepared a will leaving the Posillipo villa to his good friend Augustus. Later legend has it that upon, in turn, inheriting the villa, the Emperor Tiberius ensconced therein his lover, Alcente, with a generous gift of silver and gold. Over the ensuing centuries, this rumour led to numerous treasure-seekers digging all around the villa in the hope of finding the buried cache; they succeeded only in destroying the property. Principessa Maria remembers a séance being conducted at the villa during her father's lifetime 'just in case', but without success.

Because of its ancient Roman roots, some of the principessa's fans consider the d'Avalos estate an enclave of superb historicity. To the Principessa, however, it is simply 'my *giardino*'. She feels strongly about the magic of gardening. 'To garden is to have hope, to believe in growing things, to put your faith in the future,' she comments, with a gentle nod to Il Vesuvio, looming up directly across the bay.

Cloistered Charms

Chiostri di Santa Chiara e I Girolamini

Naples

When Goethe wrote 'Nature has lavished so many gifts on Naples, that little art is requisite to please' in his *Italian Journey* (1796), he was alluding to its spectacular setting on the Bay of Naples, its awe-inspiring backdrop of Mount Vesuvius and its delightfully clement climate. In the inner city , however, nature – in the form of parks and gardens – was hard to find and, for centuries, Naples was to count its trees as avidly as a miser counts his gold. As the city grew to be the most densely populated megalopolis of the seventeenth century (only Paris was bigger), it could only grow upwards, prevented from stretching outwards by enormous *bastioni* (city walls) constructed during the years of the Spanish vice-regality (fifteenth–seventeenth centuries). Developers could hardly find a square foot on which to build and with tenements twice the height of Paris's three-storey houses the city became a veritable human anthill.

Then, when the Bourbon kings took over in the eighteenth century, Mother Nature was completely put to rout because of the new royal tax on shade: as each tree was now taxed in order to increase income, gardens and parks became a luxury even for the Neapolitan nobility. Naples became, to quote historian Marcello Fagiolo, a garden of stone.

As a result, the city's intense urbanization did much to create a desire for nature in many of its residents, who soon fled *extra moenia* (outside the walls). In short order, Naples's environs – Sorrento, Capri and the Amalfi coast – were seeded with some of the most beautiful gardens this side of heaven.

As it turns out, it was the other side of heaven – the hereafter as promulgated by the Catholic Church – that led to some of the few pockets of greenery in Naples's centre. Thanks to the Council of Trent – whose strict Counter-Reformation reforms in the sixteenth century did so much to remake the Catholic Church – a new emphasis was placed on retreat and claustration: more than ever, monks and nuns were to live their lives behind closed doors and towering walls; and as a bit of *paradiso terrestre*, each convent and monastery was to have a cloister, and often more than one.

So, hidden behind monastery and convent walls were cloisters built to mirror the 'celestial garden'. Memories of the lost Eden, these courtyard gardens were places where monks and nuns could go for ascetic meditation. Each was centred around a well – the richer monasteries made these into lavish fountains – that was a symbol of the *fons salutis* (font of salvation).

Many of these cloistered gardens are set in the city's historic heart, the bubbling minestrone of a neighbourhood called Spaccanapoli ('split Naples'), which is built up around the 3-mile/5-kilometre-long pedestrian ribbon that cuts the inner city in two. Here, as nowhere else in the city, contrasting elements of faded gilt and romance, rust and calamity, grandeur and squalor form a dizzying stew. Shrines to the Madonna sanctify every other street corner; armies of angelic cupids cluster on sculpted marble spires called *guglie*; and every 19 September the Miracle of the Liquefaction of the Blood of St Gennaro is celebrated at the Duomo – an event said to keep Vesuvius shut down for another year. Spacca is home to some of the city's poorer residents, yet everyone looks blissful in its packed streets. Above alleyways lines of colourful laundry wave in the sun, like pennants signifying the humble dynasties teeming below. Cinderella would feel right at home.

So, too, would many of the more than ninety religious orders that built churches, monasteries and convents in the city during the fourteenth, fifteenth and sixteenth centuries, including the Jesuits, Capuchins, Franciscans, Dominicans, Augustinians and Carmelites. Among the most famous complexes is Santa Chiara, a broodingly stark Provençal Gothic church built by Robert d'Anjou, 'King Robert the Wise', between 1310 and 1328. His second wife, Sancia di Majorca, added the adjoining convent for the Poor Clares to a monastery of the Franciscan Minors.

The renowned majolica decorations on the columns and benches are the stars of the Chiostro delle Clarisse garden at Santa Chiara.

But by the eighteenth century, a secular note had entered the orders who practised strict *clausura*. Gothic was seen as too severe a style and in 1739 the abbess Ippolita Carmignani ordered the Chiostro Grande (Large Cloister) of the Santa Chiara complex to be completely redone in the newly fashionable Rococo style. The designer in charge was Domenico Antonio Vaccaro, an architect-gardener then putting the finishing touches to the Palazzo Tarsia, Naples's most extravagant private estate with a French-style garden *en parterre*.

In Santa Chiara's case, the Poor Clares were hardly that: many of the nuns came from the city's richest families. Perhaps because the sisters were homesick for all the fêtes and happiness they had left behind, Vaccaro had the cloister's eighty-two octagonal columns – which form four vine-clad pergolas that lead to two central fountains – covered with hundreds of Capodimonte tin-glazed earthenware tiles, known locally as *riggiole*. These were created by Donato and Giuseppe Massa, and painted in glowing hues of pink, green and yellow. It is hard to tell where the real vines begin and the painted garlands of vines, lemons, oranges and figs take over.

Even more delightfully, the benches that link the columns have backs showing scenes of Neapolitan life – tarantella dancers, cricket players, fishermen at the seaside, *commedia dell'arte* players – all rendered in riotous colours. Sunlight, and, in the four main parterres, roses, conifers, lemon and orange trees all add to the effect of the colourful majolica. Beginning in 2004, the cloister underwent a major restoration and most of the pergola vines were cleared away. Today, some of the horticultural magic is missing, but in another five years the arbour should return to its full glory.

A few minutes' walk from Santa Chiara leads the visitor to I Girolamini, built by the Oratorians in 1592–1619 and designed by the Florentine architect Giovanni Antonio Dosio, with neo-classical eighteenth-century additions by Ferdinando Fuga. One of the grandest church complexes in Naples, it includes the Casa dei Padri dell'Oratorio complex, entered by two cloisters. The smaller, designed by Dosio, along with Dionisio di Bartolomeo and Dionisio Lazzari, around 1600, has no vegetation at all, being a place for the monks to practise mystico-contemplative introspection. The larger is an *aranceto* (orange grove), with rows of lemon trees, pots planted with loquat trees and a central well head. Many cloisters in Naples served a practical purpose: as vineyards, *oliveti* (olive groves) or *pomaria* (apple orchards). Here, the *fraticelli* harvested their lemons. But, as with all Naples's cloisters, this one was cherished mainly as a garden to cultivate and nourish the soul.

Left: A nephrolepis fern grows atop a well head – symbolic of the fountain of life – at the centre of the smaller cloister of I Girolamini. Above: Part fruit orchard, part meditation grove, the Chiostro Grande (Large Cloister) sits at the heart of the complex of the I Girolamini Church. A Japanese medlar (*Eriobotrya japonica*) provides shade on the left, while lemon, tangerine and orange trees grow in the centre.

The Good Volcano

Giardino della Regina

Reggia di Portici

The most celebrated volcano in the world, Vesuvius proves the old adage that looks can be deceiving. A temperamental lout that has erupted hundreds of times, this 'peak of Hell rising out of Paradise' – to quote Goethe – may have finally got her annoyance out of her system on 24 August, AD 79, the fateful day when she discharged the bulk of her pent-up dyspepsia in a raging firestorm that entombed the nearby cities of Pompeii and Herculaneum. Today, Neapolitans living in the towns along the Vesuvian coast maintain a posture of grudging respect, albeit mixed with a pinch of apprehension, towards the force of nature they fondly call Il Cratere.

But they point with considerable pride to the vast fertile plains lying under the mountain, 'furrowed as by a monstrous plough' in the words of poet Gian Battista Basile. The locals may have the edge in this semantic jousting as, ecologically speaking, Campagna is one of the most fruitful areas on the planet. The slopes of Vesuvius play wet nurse to a variety of excellent wines, in particular the famous Lachryma Christi, which is second in renown only to the transcendently succulent tomato, the crown jewel among southern Italy's vegetables. And a visit to the Orto Botanico of the Reggia (Royal Palace) di Portici reveals that some of the greatest productions of Il Vesuvio have not been flames but flowers.

Triumphantly risen from the ashes of a massive lava flow in 1631, the Giardino della Regina, or Queen's Garden, remains the presiding showpiece of the Orto Botanico park and is found just east of the palace. Originally, it was part of a former *bosco regale* (royal wood) that extended from the Bay of Naples to the lower slopes of Vesuvius. The park and its palace were built for Carlo III di Bourbon and his wife, the Archduchess Maria-Amalia Cristina of Saxony, in the eighteenth century. Conceived as a Neapolitan version of Versailles,

A view of the Queen's Garden, or Giardino della Regina, from the parapet of the east front of the Bourbons' royal palace of Portici.

Left: Once topped by an antique statue of Flora excavated from nearby Herculaneum, this Fountain of Victory, sculpted by Francesco Geri, marks the centre of the Giardino della Regina. From here four walkways thread through the parterre past rare tropical trees such as the Canary palms (*Phoenix canariensis*) seen in the background. Above: Among the most prized plants in this garden, today as in the eighteenth century, are exotic cacti and succulents, such as this opuntia (a plant allied to the prickly pear or Indian fig).

the Reggia di Portici estate was designed by Antonio Canevari, who situated it to provide the king with a front-row seat at the thrilling spectacle of the then-erupting Vesuvius. The gardens – which today are the main draw – were somewhat of an afterthought, added to the estate to give the queen a stage on which to hold promenades and tea parties while the king pursued his new interest in archaeology.

The royal couple got their first taste of archaeological excitement on a visit to Portici and the seaside villa of Prince d'Elbeuf, one of the first excavators of then-buried Herculaneum. From that point on, King Carlo became avidly interested in acquiring some of the magnificent ancient Roman treasures assumed to be in the area. He issued a command to begin his own excavations in 1738, just a year after a terrific volcanic eruption had devastated the region. When ministers begged him to start digging at a safer location, Carlo shrugged off their warnings, proclaiming 'God, the immaculate Virgin, and San Gennaro will protect us.' If the worst came to pass, Carlo mused, and the royal court was buried, its remains would simply become worthy fodder for excavators working 2,000 years in the future. Fortunately, Carlo's magnificent Reggia di Portici survives intact to this day. Set with grand parterres like those created by André Le Nôtre at Versailles, the park's Giardino della Regina was designed by the Florentine Francesco Geri around a Fountain of Victory decorated with fauns and mermaids and crowned with a figure of Flora excavated from Herculaneum (but later replaced with a copy). The sculptor Giuseppe Canart earned the enmity of art historians as he was put in charge of restoring excavated sculptures, such as this Flora, from Herculaneum and often went overboard in the task.

While the overall layout of the Giardino della Regina remains the same today, the garden's plants were changed when the entire estate became part of the Royal Higher School of Agriculture, founded in 1872 and today the Orto Botanico di Portici. More than 500 species have been planted, with over 180 cacti housed in new scientific greenhouses. Key specimens include endemic plants such as the *Primula palinuri Petagna* from the Tyrrhenian coast and such exotica as *Welwitschia mirabilis*, rarely found outside its homeground of the Kalahari desert. Shadowing the magnificent nineteenth-century walled enclosure – beautifully adorned with sculpted busts and two grand ornamental portals – are many towering trees, including a spectacular *Ginkgo biloba*.

Carlo III's son, Ferdinand IV, continued to expand and enhance the royal gardens, building an imposing *castello* in the upper garden (for military exercises), a zoo and a tennis court, then a fashionable

export from Paris. He and his queen continued to give banquets here and it was at one of these in 1798 that conquering hero Admiral Horatio Nelson was introduced to Emma Hamilton, who was attending with her husband, Sir William Hamilton.

The English ambassador to the Kingdom of Naples, Sir William had become famous as an expert on Vesuvius and had made no fewer than fifty-eight explorations of the crater. He often acted as 'weatherman' in forecasting the volcano's activities to the royal monarch and his pronouncements were eagerly awaited – no one wanted to miss out on the cosmic fireworks. Today, only an occasional wisp of smoke – escaping from a hidden hillside vent – lets us know Vesuvius is down but not out. A few sceptical Neapolitans still dare to wonder: will this *détente* between the giant and civilization last? Meanwhile, possibly to make amends for her wrathful behaviour of the past, Vesuvius casts a benign influence over the surrounding fields and cities, expressed most verdantly in the exquisite gardens of the Reggia di Portici.

Above left: An outdoor nursery sheltering an array of tropical trees and plants is found behind the palace and was probably established after the Royal Higher School of Agriculture was founded here in 1872. Above right: This grand ornamental portal leads from the garden parterre to the vast *bosco royale*, or royal park, expanded during the rule of Ferdinand IV. Right: For princely collections, the more exotic the plant the better. Here, in the foreground, is a *Grevillea juniperina*, hailing from Australia and shadowed by one of the garden's towering Canary palms (*Phoenix canariensis*).

Through English Eyes

Villa Lanzara

Nocera

Personality is as unmistakable in gardens as in human beings, and each is equally influenced by the prevailing environment. The naturalistic gardens of the late eighteenth-century are a case in point. For centuries, extravagant window dressing in the form of pomp and panoply had made gardens serve as reflections of royal power, ducal courts and imperial whim. In France during the reign of Louis XIV even Mother Nature took a back seat to the ruler-straight allées, formal terracing and clipped parterres that André Le Nôtre had installed at Versailles. But these rigid traditions began to crumble when France's young queen Marie-Antoinette constructed a miniature mock-farm – complete with imported sheep and a garden laid out in the new English manner – in a corner of the palace grounds. Banished were Versailles's strict 'green geometries', and in their stead appeared hidden nooks, a wayward brook, meandering paths and a pretty Temple of Love.

Happy to exchange diamonds for dewdrops, the queen would retreat to her little playground, the Hameau, to frolic with other young ladies and stroll through its secluded park and gardens where, away from the unfriendly eyes of Louis's court, the still-girlish 'Toinette' was free to answer Rousseau's 'call to Nature', wherein simple qualities like emotion and sentiment could flower.

It wasn't long before Marie-Antoinette's sister, Queen Maria-Carolina, had her own English-style garden installed at the Reggia di Caserta, the royal palace 20 miles/32 kilometres north of Naples, laid out by John Anthony Graefer. The new English fashion soon influenced Italian gardens everywhere, and when Graefer died prematurely in 1815, his three sons took over and helped promulgate the *giardino all'inglese*. Historians believe that John, Carl or George Graefer took on the role of designer of the enchanting garden of the Villa Lanzara.

The villa's grounds were once part of the vast Reggia Borbonica – the estate of the Bourbon kings, prized for its hunting and agricultural facilities and extending northward more than 50 miles/80 kilometres to the great palace of Caserta. Goethe became familiar with the area on his many trips to Vesuvius and praised its fertility and scenic beauty in his *Italian Journey* (1816). The villa was constructed in Nocera Superiore (in the upper town's pretty *località* called Croce dei Malloni) by the Calenda family, members of the royal court, during the late eighteenth century. By 1820, the villa had been sold to Andrea Lanzara, ancestor of the present proprietress, Countess Cettina Lanzara.

Today, the garden remains an extraordinary fusion of styles: it may speak the Italian language but it does so with a strikingly British accent.

A delightful hybrid, it is Mediterranean in the exotic species of banana and rare palm trees, formal white statuary and notable prominence of southern blooms, including more than twenty-five species of camellias, and English in the 'careful carelessness' of its winding paths, mixed flower beds, grand yews and Regency-style coffee house smothered with ivy.

Past a graceful white wrought-iron gate, a soaring 80-foot/34-metre-tall *Washingtonia robusta* palm delivers the main wow factor of the garden. Forming a telling contrast to this South American treasure are the encircling *Trachelospermum jasminoides* and velvet belt of mossy grass. Another indication of the English taste of this garden is that it is extremely lawn conscious. Lawns were the most fashionable elements of British gardens: for pure horticultural snobbery they couldn't be beaten because of the high costs of the plentiful watering and constant maintenance they needed.

Near by, flower beds containing fuchsias and violets form a

As if playing hide-and-seek amid holm oaks, bushes of pittosporum and blooms of white acanthus, a statue of Hebe surprises anyone strolling along the curving path laid out in the eighteenth-century English manner.

floral mosaic to rival the splendours inside the Byzantine domes of Ravenna. But as you stroll up the seductively curving main path, you note that its border of convallaria is moderated by the hoary green hue of the stately yew trees and holm oaks that line the path. Here and there the eye is caught by some of the beautiful camellias in the garden, including *C. japonica* 'Adolphe Audusson' and *C.j.* 'Alba Simplex'. Everywhere there are *Pinus pinea*, which, even in the bright spring, sober the gaiety of flowers such as *Salvia splendens*, yet these grand old pines, so stern and joyless, seem to wear a smile, like age wooed by rosy childhood, thanks to these colourful flowers.

Other parts of the garden can be discovered by following winding trails. Deliciously covered with verdure, and passing under curtains of holm oaks and through carpets of spring flowers, the paths lead to hidden surprises: a Bath of Venus grotto, an orangery and, finally, the epitome of the style *all'inglese*: a coffee-house pavilion.

Inside this there are remnants of spectacular Giustiniani majolica tilework; outside, the entire exterior wears a raiment of gorgeous English ivy, beautifully coiffured and sculpted by the pruning knife. Here one can imagine ladies of the day hiding from the noonday sun over coffee served in Sèvres china, and enjoying platters of fresh strawberries and pitchers of cream, while discreetly revelling in the latest poems by Byron. Take away the American *Aloe margina*, the Himalayan pine and the *Phoenix reclinata*, add a few young ladies in Empire-style frocks and plumed bonnets, and to a garden-lover endowed with romantic tendencies and a capacity to ignore the proximity of Vesuvius, this spot might be in England itself.

Above left: While the garden is largely a symphony of greens, spectacular flowers such as this calla lily lend spots of colour. Above centre: An array of potted plants seems to form a 'bed' of coleus varieties. Above right: A wonderland oasis of greenery, the garden offers only glimpses of the outside world, such as this one of the eighteenth-century 'medieval' tower of the Villa Lanzara.

When Knighthood Was in Flower

Castello Lancellotti

Lauro

*A*s you drive up the gravel road to the machiolated gateway of the Castello Lancellotti, you sense a heady perfume in the air. There are no rose bushes in sight, no stone walls vested with jasmine; instead, you are breathing deep the extraordinary historical fragrance of the fairest, if not oldest, castle in Campania. Set on a lofty rock and lording it over the entire Vallo di Lauro, the *castello* looks almost the same today as it did a thousand years ago. Archival documents allow scholars to trace its venerable ownership back to the Longobard era (tenth and eleventh centuries), the Norman kingdom (twelfth century), the Angevin age (thirteenth and fourteenth centuries) and the Aragonese viceroyship (fourteenth and fifteenth centuries); in the sixteenth century it belonged to the Princes Pignatelli, and the Princes Lancellotti have owned it since 1615. Married into the Aldobrandini and Lante della Rovere families, the Lancellotti were one of the greatest dynastic clans of Rome and had the finest archaeological collection of the day to prove it.

Bristling with Guelf towers, impregnable keeps and frowning battlements, the castle looks like an illumination from a medieval missal – but appearances can be deceiving. In truth, the entire complex is a romantic reconstruction created after the original Lombard–Norman castle burned to the ground on 30 April 1799 after it was sacked by Napoleon's marauding troops on their way to put an end to the short-lived Parthenopean Republic (an attempt to put the deposed Ferdinand IV back on his Neapolitan throne).

In 1872, inspired by the nineteenth-century vogue for medievalism, Prince Pietro Massimo Lancellotti decided to reconstruct his ancient family seat. And the key to making all the dead centuries come alive again was the flowering gardens that were once more to form the heart of the castle.

A view from the Renaissance-style loggetta reveals the castle's inner courtyard with its Upper and Lower Gardens.

For within these brooding walls glow two gardens, reconstructions of the Renaissance originals. Past the portcullis of the outer courtyard – a vast stone *piazzale* that once functioned as a parade ground and stableyard – the inner courtyard is divided in half. Shadowed by the towering Romanesque-style campanile of the castle chapel is the Upper Garden, designed around a sixteenth-century fountain, fed by nearby rainwater-collecting basins lined with decorative majolica tiles and planted with pleached mandarin-orange (*Citrus reticulata*) trees – an allusion to the fruit that adorns the *stemma* (family crest) of the Pignatellis. A grassy path lined by hedges of *Laurus nobilis* and *Prunus laurocerasus* weaves its way around the fountain, its gentle curves reflecting the late-nineteenth-century romantic vogue for walks for the *pensieroso* – the contemplative stroller – instead of perfectly symmetrical paths. Adding beauty here are also a centuries-old coral tree (*Erythrina crista-galli*) and plantings of myrtle (*Myrtus communis*), *Lagerstroemia indica* and *Camellia japonica*.

Almost hidden from this vantage point is the Lower Garden, laid out on a terrace a full flight of steps below and accessed only by stone staircases. Crammed with myriad shapes sculpted out of box (*Buxus sempervirens*), this *giardino all'italiana* has the distinction of being the best surviving topiary garden of Campania. While many consider topiary an English art form, historians place it in the Italian

Renaissance revival of classical antiquity. Alberti, the fifteenth-century Tuscan scholar and archaeologist, not only rediscovered ancient Greek myths but also took a page out of Pliny's book and dusted off the art of the Roman *topiarius*, effectively restoring clipped yew hedges and box trees to the roles they had filled in the gardens of the ancient emperors. By the sixteenth century, the *arte topiaria* had become the most fashionable garden style in Italy, and in Campania, it found its most famous example at Poggio Reale, a vast villa that was one of the largest royal estates in Naples, but neither this, nor the formal gardens of other Neapolitan court abodes, such as the Castel Capuano and the Castel Nuovo, still exist.

Looking more built than planted, the perfectly smooth-clipped shapes of the Lower Garden compress much into little. The paths are extremely narrow, a clever device to guide unsuspecting sixteenth-century visitors along their merry way until they were surprised by being splashed with water from the garden's hidden fountains. The fountains were supplied by the marble-clad *pescheria* (fish pond) that stands in one corner of the garden, once part of an impressive 'antique' nymphaeum (or *ninfeo*) that helped cool overheated guests.

The *giochi d'acqua* (water games) remind us that by the mid-sixteenth century, the knight in leather, buckram and clanking steel had given way to the *galantuomo* swathed in rich brocades, gold

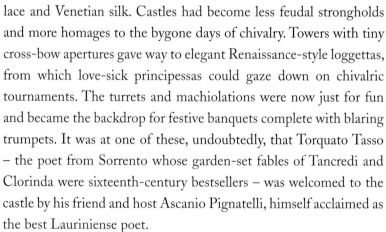

lace and Venetian silk. Castles had become less feudal strongholds and more homages to the bygone days of chivalry. Towers with tiny cross-bow apertures gave way to elegant Renaissance-style loggettas, from which love-sick principessas could gaze down on chivalric tournaments. The turrets and machiolations were now just for fun and became the backdrop for festive banquets complete with blaring trumpets. It was at one of these, undoubtedly, that Torquato Tasso – the poet from Sorrento whose garden-set fables of Tancredi and Clorinda were sixteenth-century bestsellers – was welcomed to the castle by his friend and host Ascanio Pignatelli, himself acclaimed as the best Lauriniense poet.

Today, the viols still strum, at the summertime Renaissance-style *manifestazione-spettacolo* hosted by the current owner, Prince Pietro Lancellotti. With tumbling jesters, standard-bearing heralds and court pages recreating flambeaux-lit scenes from the Crusades out of Tasso's *Jerusalem Delivered* within the castle gardens, these evenings are always sold out – proof that the interest in medievalism and its courtly spectacles of pomp and ceremony is as intense today as it was with the nostalgic courtiers of the sixteenth century.

Above left and overleaf: Once the centre of a full-scale Renaissance nymphaeum, the *pescheria* (fish pond) remains the main water supply for the entire garden. Above centre: The castle's topiary garden is one of the last extant examples of the sixteenth-century *giardino all'italiana*, whose sculpted box shapes were meant to recall the gardens of classical antiquity. Designed to be viewed to best advantage from the arcaded gallery, hidden water jets were secreted in the garden – a surprise way of cooling unsuspecting guests. Above right: Pleached mandarin-orange trees shade the Upper Garden, as this fruit adorned the family *stemma* of the Pignatellis, former benefactors of the castle's magnificent chapel.

The Global Garden

Orto Botanico

Naples

*B*y the mid-point of the eighteenth century, the city of Naples beckoned as an essential stop on the Grand Tour. Its value as gateway to the ancient treasures of Pompeii and the awesome presence of Mount Vesuvius, combined with rumours of panoramic sea views, a heavenly climate and historic architecture, made the city irresistible to travellers. Heavily represented in the first wave of these were kings, queens and dukes, as well as the cream of Europe's *gran turisti*. At the same time another circuit was evolving, this one heading out to the farthest corners of the globe and inspired by the great voyages of discovery of the fifteenth and sixteenth centuries. For these travellers, souvenirs were not antique marbles or remnants of gilded mosaics. Instead, they shipped home dragon trees, bird-of-paradise orchids and exotic cacti; the greater the strangeness factor, the more desirable the plant specimen. The horticultural collections that resulted were natural extensions of the *wunderkammer* – 'collections of wonders' – that had been added to many palaces during the Baroque era.

While a few *gran signori* of boundless wealth had the means to fund such expeditions, it was most often through the power and privileges of royalty that horticultural exotica were introduced to gardens. In 1796, Ferdinand IV decreed that the botanist Giovanni Pianelli and the architect Francesco Maresca would create a royal botanical garden in Naples. As fate would have it, though, the Neapolitan kingdom was forfeited to the French after a populist uprising – later known as the Parthenopean Republic – cleared the way for Joseph Bonaparte, Napoleon's brother, to take the throne, and the idea languished. In the manner of kingly succession that is all too characteristic of turbulent times, Joseph was replaced as king of Naples by Napoleon's brother-in-law, General Joachim Murat (Joseph being given a sidewise promotion to the throne of Spain).

A view into the garden's fernery, an cool oasis of luxuriant, shady foliage. Ferneries had become a leading fashion in Victorian gardens and one especially cultivated in hot Mediterranean climes.

During Murat's short reign (1808–15), significant democratic reforms championing the values of *liberté, fraternité et egalité* were passed, ranging from schools for the general populace to the construction of higher educational facilities. One result of the reforms, mandated by Murat on 19 February 1810, was that the idea of creating a royal garden was resurrected.

Between 1808 and 1812, 30 acres/12 hectares were requisitioned in La Sanità, which is set at the foot of the Capodimonte hill and is still one of the more Hogarthian backwaters of the city. The eastern border of the new Orto Botanico (Botanical Garden) was created by the Albergo dei Poveri, the erstwhile poorhouse of the city (the former Palazzo Fuga, which remains one of the largest structures in Europe). The southern border, running along Via Forio, comprised a massive wall, a gate and a ceremonial double stairway, all built – this was around 1815, following the return to power of the Bourbons – by Vincenzo Paolotti and based on designs by Giuliano de Fazio. The foundation specimens of the garden were provided by the purchase of exotic collections amassed by the Marchese of Gravina from his estate at Bellavista and the Prince of Bisignano from his estate in Barra. The new garden was entrusted to the spectacularly capable hands of Michele Tenore (1780–1861), who would retain the post of *capo giardiniere* for the next fifty years. His claim to horticultural glory lies in his *Flora Napolitana*, a monumental five-volume work dated 1816, which described 400 new species and 3,400 vascular plants indigenous to the kingdom of Naples.

Since plant collecting had become an obsession for royalty and fashionable aristocrats, the new Orto Botanico was to showcase foreign species: it was to be a kind of passepartout to the entire world of horticulture. The horticultural commoners of Campania, such as *Quercus ilex* and *Arbutus unedo*, bowed low to camellia bushes from Japan, pink frangipani from the Costa Rican jungle and Douglas firs from North America.

Thus when you walk up the central Viale Domenico Cirillo, a vast amphitheatrical display opens up of cacti and succulents such as aloes and opuntias (all share the common characteristic of storing water, of great interest in a region like Campania where water has long been more precious than gold). To make this Desert Garden as attractive to sightseers as to scientists, it is both studiously informative – labels describe the plant families, including Cactaceae, Euphorbiaceae, Aloaceae and Agavaceae, while the garden is laid out to show the plants' relationships – and beautiful enough, thanks to giant boulders and sculpted sand patches. Near by, in a telling contrast, is a reflecting pool planted with aquatic species ranging

Above: The first greenhouse of the Orto, the Merola Greenhouse – La Serra Monumentale – was built in 1820 in neo-classical style, replete with Doric columns and carved metopes. Right: The central allée of the garden opens up to an amphitheatrical Desert Garden – a spectacular display of cacti and succulents that hail mainly from North America. In a region where water was more precious than gold, these plants were especially prized. Here they have been stage-arranged around sand strands and giant boulders.

from *Mentha aquatica* and water lilies to the floating fern *Azolla filiculoides*.

To the right of the central boulevard, there are spectacular trees, such as a pagoda tree (*Parrotia persica*) from Iran and the Australian *Melaleuca styphelioides*, one of the first examples planted in Italy, and a cool, humid fernery, the diametric opposite of the cacti display. Although it dates only to the 1950s, the fernery comprises many species popular in the Victorian era, when seemingly every home had a corner devoted to the swaying fronds. The display includes

examples of beech fern, oak fern, lady fern, maidenhair, hard fern, spleenwort, rusty-back and, visible in one of the shaded thickets, the rare *Woodwardia radicans*. Like its manmade counterpart, the hand-held fan, a fern always looks invitingly cool, so it is no wonder that under Campania's unrelenting sun there were many fern fanciers.

Rising up towards the back of the garden are the Orto's two main structures. To the west stands La Serra Monumentale (the Merola Greenhouse), which was built in neo-classical style in around 1820, with a façade of Doric columns and topped by thirty metopes, with carvings of the most fashionable plant species of the early nineteenth century. There are four other greenhouses, where shrubs, herbaceous and arboreous species are cultivated. Not far from La Serra Monumentale is the Palm Grove, where pride of place goes to the *Cycas revoluta* given to the Orto in 1813 by Queen Maria-Carolina, wife of Joachim Murat and sister of Napoleon. Once she and her king were forced from the throne of Naples in 1815, the Bourbon king Ferdinand II returned, and he ordered a grove of Asian *Citrus* species to be planted around the *castello* that towers over the western corner of the Orto. The curators here point to trees bearing multi-coloured 'German breeches' fruit or those laden with lemons with 'turmoil of Venus' peels. The *castello*, a mock-Gothic fortress, is now home to the garden's Paleobotanic and Ethnobotanic Museums. Outside the *castello*'s portal blooms a huge *Camellia japonica*; inside its courtyard stands an impressive *Gardenia thunbergia* from South Africa.

Today the Orto Botanico caters to several distinct audiences. For botanists, it is an important adjunct to the science division of Naples's Universita di Federico II. The garden's comprehensive plant collection – numbering some 25,000 examples of 10,000 species – also serves as a living laboratory for the vast floral industry that helps power Campania, the fourth largest flower grower in Italy. In addition, for serious plant collectors and scholars the Orto is a 'Louvre' of nineteenth-century horticulture. But perhaps the botanical garden finds its greatest value in being an escape valve in an overcrowded city. Beautiful enough for an afternoon-long stroll *nel verde* (in green), the Orto Botanico di Napoli remains an island of tranquillity and ecological peace in the heart of one of Italy's most teeming centres.

Above: While several greenhouses of the Orto house prize specimens from its huge cycads collection, others are grown in the open air, here rubbing shoulders with other conifers. Right: The rare and the regional often grow side by side at the Orto, such as these fantastic specimens of Mexican fan palm (*Washingtonia robusta*) and holm oak (*Quercus ilex*) seen in the foreground. Set off to perfection by the green setting is the garden's mock-Gothic *castello*.

Along the Golden Mile
Villa De Gregorio di Sant'Elia
Portici

Left: Whether it is her winter camellias or summer roses, Principessa De Gregorio di Sant'Elia always has flowers that echo the corals and terracottas of her nineteenth-century neo-Gothic villa. Above: Climbing alongside the grand stone staircases leading to the Upper Garden are bushes of ivy and magnolia.

*B*y nature, gardeners live in the future: they are planting for the years to come. To them, flowers are friendly conspirators who help them forget the pace of time. But what if a garden is haunted by its own history – of, say, 200 years? This is true of a repository of Neapolitan flora in Portici, Italy, namely the Villa De Gregorio di Sant'Elia, the only garden in Naples for which the original map – showing the exact location of every plant – and seasonal plan still exist.

This issue of historical relevance confronts Principessa Uzza De Gregorio di Sant'Elia every spring, when her garden-park bursts into extravagant bloom. With a twinkle in her eye, she likes to protest that she 'has no time for ghosts': there are too many nursemaids and grandchildren, too many family and garden-society fêtes to arrange. At the same time, she readily acknowledges that her garden is virtually a museum. Indeed, her role as overseer is equivalent to that of a museum curator, as she is required to notify the local municipal council, the Superintendenza di Portici, if ever a vine of her blue *Plumbago capensis* dies or if she has to cut off a dead branch of a 'Lady Hume's Blush' magnolia. And she always remains true to the garden's historic blueprint: 'I try to plant the same plants as indicated in the eighteenth-century map of the garden, which is a great help. If I have to replace old plants, I make an effort to work with seedlings from growths already in the garden, rather than obtaining them from a supplier.' After more than fifty years under her loving care and authority, which began when she married into the Cattaneo family, her bounteous beds of agapanthus still flourish and her towering holm oaks continue to acquire grandeur as they age. Today, she continues to rule over her 20-acre/8-hectare kingdom with a kind but firm hand.

As a result, the Villa De Gregorio has survived and flourished. This is all the more remarkable as it is set in one of the most densely populated districts in all Italy. Ringed with walls and 40-foot/ 12-metre holm oak trees, however, the estate is an island of green

serenity, and it is the finest specimen of the Ville Vesuviana – villas built in the eighteenth century along the Miglio d'Oro (Golden Mile) district – and the only one of the thirty extant structures still inhabited by the family who built it.

During the Neapolitan Golden Age – 1734 to 1805 – Carlo III and later, his son, Ferdinand IV, employed the art of architecture and the wiles of decoration to transform Naples from a squalid backwater into a resplendent city. Charles's involvement with the process introduced him to the beguiling Arcadian landscape and mild climate of the adjacent region of the Vesuvian Riviera – the stretch of coastland between the Bay of Naples and Vesuvius – and he decided to erect a palace there, the sumptuous Reggia di Portici. The area was not far from one of the world's other most-talked-about spots, Pompeii, where ongoing excavations were about to unleash a vogue for the neo-classical style. Charles paid no heed that his new palace was being built too near the volatile Vesuvius. Before long, the royal 'we' had swelled to an army of courtiers, who set about constructing a spate of villas around the Reggia, like satellites attending a sun. By the

mid-eighteenth century, the Miglio d'Oro, from Portici to Torre del Greco, was lined with villas graced with elaborate gardens whose allées, vistas, follies, floriettas, pergolas, fountains, pools and statuary served as backdrops for entertainments, balls and concerts. Today, most of the magic of that era has evaporated, many of the villas having been lost to the scythe of progress. There remain only about ten, which, though dim shadows of their former glorious selves, have been protected since 1971 by the Ente per le Ville Vesuviane association.

When the principessa's husband's forebear Baldassare Cattaneo purchased the property where the villa now stands in 1650, it consisted of a simple Neapolitan country house, a *casa di campagna*. Fortune smiled warmly on the Cattaneos and by the mid-eighteenth century one of Baldassare's descendants, Domenico, had risen to become the Principe di San Nicandro and, more influentially, *precettore* (tutor) to Ferdinand IV, the son of Carlo VII. At the age of eight, when Carlo chose to leave for the prospect of greater glory in Spain, the boy was named heir-designate to the throne of the Kingdom of the Two Sicilies and until he reached the age of sixteen, Naples was ruled by

a regency council, in part led by Domenico Cattaneo.

Finding that his family property was just a short carriage ride from the Portici palace, the Principe di San Nicastro engaged the premier architect of the day, Luigi Vanvitelli, to build him a residence befitting his newly exalted status. Soon the plain-and-simple *casa di campagna* was replaced by a suitably regal edifice, the Villa De Gregorio di Sant'Elia. Its majestic façade was adorned with two-storey-high pilasters, and a curved rusticated exedra wall was embellished with statuary enclosed in niches (scholars say this was a trial run for the garden exedra of Eolo, which Vanvitelli built in 1781 at Carlo VII's mammoth palace at Caserta). The Cattaneo gene for property improvement apparently lay dormant for about a century, until Domenico's heir, Giulia Cattaneo, who was married to the Duca di Pignatelli Aragona Cortes – of one of the great families of Naples – added a wing in the new Romantic style then becoming fashionable. Designed by Nicola Breglia in 1866, this has two castellated towers constructed of bands of coral- and terracotta-hued stone. Inside, the reception rooms were furnished with gilt mirrors,

Above left: Along with camellias and roses, geraniums add spots of colour to the verdantly green garden. Above centre: In this garden almost all the borders are formed by African lilies (*Agapanthus africanus*). Above right: Many of the moss-covered stone urns of the garden are planted with cordylines.

Victorian étagères, Turkish tiles and, in keeping with the owners' high status and wealth, the first gas-lit lamps in Campania. As the family had by now switched their allegiance from the Bourbons to Italy's royal House of Savoy (unlike most Neapolitan aristos), their 'new' villa was inaugurated by no less a personage than Crown Prince Vittorio Emanuele III.

Despite the many velvet-cushioned salons available to Principessa Uzza, her favourite 'room' remains the garden, through which she relishes taking visitors. Always elegantly coiffed and often wearing a simple but *molto* chic white sheath – which helps her stand out among the colourful flowers and greenery – she usually begins the tour in the English Garden. Its simple lawn, considered a luxury in the nineteenth century because of its need for constant upkeep and water, is bordered by a famous collection of camellias; prize specimens include the white 'Duchess of Orleans', the pink scarlet 'Great Sultan' and the carmine-tinged 'Contessa Lavinia Maggi'. The blaze of the camellias' reds is calmed by a selection of yellow mimosa planted below. Beyond lies a parterre set with a circular pool, surrounded by four piperno benches, each crowned by a terracotta bust of a goddess and framed by beds of agapanthus and *Magnolia grandiflora* 'Gallissonnière'. From here a stone staircase inset with a Baroque fountain takes you up to an ivy-covered bridge that leads to a charming 'folly' of a miniature ruined castle. Forming a green backdrop is a community of oak and eucalyptus trees, plus a variety of palm trees, including *Cycas revoluta*, *Ginkgo biloba*, *Washingtonia robusta*, *Chamaerops humils* and *Phoenix reclinata*, all of which lend this so-called 'English' garden a somewhat exotic, appropriately Campanian touch.

After you leave the shadowy knolls and winding paths of this area, a gigantic swath of greensward welcomes you to the Italian Garden. This is presided over by an imposing nineteenth-century greenhouse designed by Breglia, which echoes his Galleria Principi di Napoli, a famed glass-and-cast-iron covered arcade erected on Naples's Via Pessina in 1869. Beyond the greenhouse a vast parterre opens up, a pattern of privet hedges which contain constellations of indigo-blue agapanthus and 'Blue Bird' hydrangea.

An observer on one of her tours will sense that the principessa knows every tree – 'many are them are old friends' – and practically even every twig and leaf. Seeing that a branch of a 50-foot/15-metre-tall holm oak needs to be removed, she makes a note to call the local fire department. A tour usually ends by the gigantic pool – her one concession to modernity – that she had installed for the use of her grandchildren. Sitting beside it, a glass pitcher of iced lemonade at hand, the principessa turns contemplative. 'Problems? Everything! Pruning! Sick plants! Ageing trees! I can understand my children's view that this garden may be too "cumbrous". One has to admit that conservation – our keynote – and trying to keep up with the garden's history is a great challenge.'

Who will take on the onerous responsibility of maintaining the estate and gardens in the future remains to be seen – her children, or some conservation-minded agency? – but whether or not we ourselves are gardeners, just being made aware of the principessa's labours is sufficient to add us to the list of honorary 'inheritors' of the gardens of the Villa De Gregorio di Sant'Elia.

Above: Around the fountain of the English Garden are abundant plantings of magnolia, holm oak and camellia. Right: Agapanthus is also used as an edging plant in the English Garden, where lawns were the stellar attraction in the nineteenth century, when they were the ultimate luxury because of their constant need for water and upkeep.

II

❧

Treasured Islands

Capri and Ischia

How Greene Was His Island

Villa Il Rosaio

Anacapri

The weight of words that have been written about Capri is enormous: the rapturous chronicles of the travel writers, the novels, the poems, the stories. Over the centuries, this beautiful Bali Hai in the Bay of Naples has received every rave; every encomium has been used, every superlative proclaimed. Perhaps that is why Graham Greene, Capri's most famous writer in residence, never wrote – and barely uttered – a syllable about his adopted home.

In one interview, however, he stated, 'It really isn't my kind of place.' And the Capri that is the milieu of the chic, the glamorous harbourage of billionaire yachts and the stage for Hollywooden parties was not. But the silver lining to the cloud that shrouds the Siren Heights of the island is Anacapri: the tranquil, charming town perched on the slopes of Monte Solaro. There, with his profits from *The Third Man*, Greene bought the Villa Il Rosaio, an estate located in the labyrinth of streets running off Piazza Caprile, Anacapri's central square. From 1948 on, for forty years, Greene climbed the hill to the villa each spring and autumn, returning again and again as though to an old affair. What he found inside its gates would make anyone fall in love.

Hidden behind towering walls smothered in bougainvillea, and small enough to covet, the villa is a two-storey *casa mediterranea* built in the vernacular 'peasant' Caprese style. Surrounding it are an adorably cosy *letto-studiolo* , a raised portico, a magnificent vine-clad pergola and tiny paths threading through three terraced gardens. The latter are so deftly and delightfully woven throughout the property they seem to underscore those writers who have pointed out that the mere act of walking has become an 'art' on Capri. Like the rose bush after which it is named, Il Rosaio seems to have grown organically into an array of toy-sized delights, reminding us that we are impressed by the smallness of everything on Capri (even the size of its main square, Il Piazzetta); Il Rosaio, like much of Capri, has a general air of make-believe.

In this case, the magician was Capri's most celebrated designer of houses and gardens, Edwin Cerio, one-time mayor of the island (1920–23). Conservationist *par excellence*, he was alarmed that the isle was being engulfed by a rising tide of the chi-chi homes of international sybarites. Leading culprits were the Villa Lysis, Baron Fersen's gilded essay in Belle Epoque style, and the Villa Monte San Michele, Lady Blanche Gordon-Lennox's botanical extravaganza, which overflowed with trees and flowers from far-flung lands. During the 1920s, '30s and '40s, Cerio graced the island with its most coveted domiciles, including the Villa Il Solario, Il Studio and Il Monacone, and worked hard to conserve the island's native species.

To help build his case for the preservation of traditional Caprese architecture, Cerio set about creating Il Rosaio. It had begun life as a simple peasant's house, owned by Edith Hempsted, reputed to be the illegitimate daughter of Edward VII of England. As a *piccolo eremo* (little hermitage) it had welcomed a series of illustrious guests, including the novelist Compton Mackenzie (who wrote *Sinister Street* there between 1914 and 1916), the composer Ottorino Respighi (who composed *Boutique Fantasque* for Diaghilev's Ballets Russes here in 1919) and the writer Francis Brett Young (who wrote *The Black Diamond* here in 1920).

Beginning in 1921, Cerio first added Il Bocciuolo, a tiny studio like a sailor's cabin (Cerio was also a former naval engineer). This little room with a desk and a bed was where Greene would write major parts of *The End of the Affair*, *The Quiet American*, *Our Man in Havana* and *Travels with my Aunt*. Next, Cerio enlarged the main house, La Rosa, with a raised balcony-portico adorned with terracotta

The quintessence of Caprese style, Il Rosaio is the masterpiece of Edwin Cerio, Capri's leading designer of houses and gardens. Here, his white-on-white architecture offers an eye-catching backdrop to geraniums, agaves, a *Magnolia grandiflora* tree and – draped over the archetypal column-and-timber pergola – radiant bougainvillea.

jars. Connecting the two little houses he made a spectacular pergola in typical Caprese style, with white columns supporting wooden slates, over which vines were trained.

In this manner, Cerio transformed the property into a tiny *villaggio*, complete with walkways of rose-coloured *pavimento* and sculpturesque elements such as little cupolas and lanterns (which had taken their architectural cue from the nearby district called Le Boffre, where the houses had groined barrel vaults that look like 'swellings', called *boffre* in the Neapolitan dialect). But the main spell of the property emanated from the garden.

A stepped path leads past a wall covered with espaliered roses to the main vine-draped pergola, from which you can see the entire extent of the estate as it winds its way down the three stepped terraces. On the first terrace, plumbago and lantana parade their colours against walls sculpted to hold *panca* (benches), inspired by those in the *all'antica* paintings of Alma-Tadema. The ancient Roman 'look' is also underlined with an array of giant amphorae, overflowing with red-pink geraniums and bougainvillea. Near by sits an ancient olive-oil press, similar to one preserved in the Museo

Opposite: Glimpsed through the trumpet-shaped angel's tears (*Brugmansia suaveolens*) and the violet flowers of wisteria are the lower patio and poolside lawn. Above left: All the magic of Capri is compressed into one tiny cul-de-sac, thanks to a coloured *pavimento*, a built-in *panca* or bench, an ogival wall and a classic arbour for bougainvillea, geraniums and roses. Above right: Protected by a line of sentinel cypresses, an outdoor dining/writing area is accessed past a magnificent *Agave americana* and a sculpted stucco balustrade.

Archaeologico Nazionale in Naples. Steps lead down to the second terrace, which is graced with myrtle and rosemary. The bottom level is a beautiful lawn, where blue convolvulus is trained up the trunks of two hoary olive trees, which shade a lovely pool, and a rose bed adds scent.

The only thorn to this rose was, as it turns out, Graham Greene himself, at least according to Shirley Hazard, whose memoir *Greene on Capri* (Virago, 2000) paints a picture of the author as a prickly, whining, short-tempered man who had little or no appreciation of the visual splendour of the island. Other than restaurant dinners at La Gemma, strolls to the Belvedere Migliera and after-hours cocktails on Il Piazzetta, Hazard sees him playing no major part in the Pirandello plot of life on Capri. But seeing the total enchantment of his garden makes you understand why he rarely left his Anacapri home, where, he said, 'in four weeks I do the work of six months elsewhere'. A parting look at this revivifying, floriferous garden – now magnificently restored by the lucky owner since 1990, the noted lawyer Francesco Ricci – underscores how much mental nectar an England-weary Greene distilled from his Rosaio.

Having bought the villa, Signor Ricci was intent on leaving intact this quintessential example of Cerio's 'Capri style'. If parts of the house needed little restoration – in the Bocciuolo you'll find Greene's own Olivetti 22 sitting on the workbench where he left it – the garden was in a sad state, perhaps understandably so, since Greene only lived here for several months a year during a thirty-year span. Other than installing a pool on the lowest level of the garden, the property is just as Cerio imagined it. 'As Cerio designed both the house and the garden,' Signor Ricci points out, 'they seem to merge, magically, into one entity.' His total commitment to the renaissance of the garden even led him to restore the large cistern, constructed with stone and *lapili*, a type of work that has now disappeared, to collect rainwater. 'It may be, in fact, the only tank of that type on the island: the few that survived have now all been converted into apartments.' Enjoying the garden during a May sunset, when Ricci believes the garden's magic is most potent, it is easy to believe that Villa Il Rosaio is the most beguiling, most bewitching little garden in the world.

Left and right: In a style borrowed from the adjacent Le Boffre neighbourhood – sculpted as if from *zabaglione* – white stucco was moulded by Cerio into little cupolas, lanterns, pedestals and a dazzling array of *terrazzi*, transforming 'The Rosebush' into Capri's most adorable stage set.

Seeds of Inspiration
La Mortella

Ischia

'I forget why we came here: Ischia. It was being very much talked about, though few people seemed actually to have seen it – except, perhaps, as a jagged blue shadow glimpsed across the water from the heights of its celebrated neighbor, Capri. Some people advised against Ischia and, as I remember, they gave rather spooky reasons: you realize that there is an active volcano?' When Truman Capote wrote these words for *Mademoiselle* in 1950, Ischia was, indeed, *terra incognita* to all but a few intrepid travellers. Then colonized only by goatherds and wine growers, the island is presided over by Mount Epomeo, a now-quiescent volcano which once sculpted the island's raggedly beautiful landscape. With hillsides perfumed by broom and lavender, prettified by wild cyclamen, arbutus and violets, and studded with gigantic volcanic rocks that Capote likened to 'sleeping dinosaurs', Ischia continues today to captivate many visitors to this part of Campania.

Thanks to travellers' praise – 'what a strange, and strangely enchanted, place this is: an encantada in the Mediterranean,' Capote wrote to friends (as quoted in Gerald Clarke's *Too Brief a Treat: The Letters of Truman Capote*) – boatloads of pioneering holidaymakers had begun arriving. Prominent among them were Sir William Walton and his young bride, Susana. Hailed as Britain's brightest composer – he created such works as *Façade*, *Belshazzar's Feast* and the soundtrack for Laurence Olivier's *Henry V*, *Hamlet* and *Richard III* – Walton was seeking a respite from London's frantic pace. He decided that he had found what he was seeking in the languid tempo of Forio, Ischia's second-largest town, and returned in 1956 to make his home there. At first glance, the Waltons' newly acquired property – they called it La Mortella after the 'divine myrtle' blanketing the hillsides – held little promise. On viewing it, Sir Laurence tut-tutted, 'You'll never make anything of this.' And he had a point: could such a jumble of volcanic leftovers – knobbly protrusions of rock, arid gulleys, acres of dying olive and chestnut trees – be transformed into the hoped-for Eden?

To thousands of garden-lovers who adoringly seek out La Mortella every year, the answer is a resounding yes. The amazing transformation of yesteryear's jumble into today's extraordinary fusion of art and nature is a tribute to the intuitive genius of Sir William, Lady Susana – Walton's muse, and until her passing in 2010, the unofficial 'patron saint' of the island – and, not least, their brilliant landscape architect, Russell Page. Later, Page was invited to wave his horticultural wand over properties owned by such clients as the Duke and Duchess of Windsor, New York society's Babe Paley, Giovanni and Marella Agnelli, and Oscar de la Renta – and came to be hailed as one of the most influential garden designers of the twentieth century.

Page's endeavours at La Mortella achieved two seemingly opposing ends: while staying true to the natural characteristics of the island, he at the same time created a unique atmosphere, unlike anything most gardeners had ever seen. The garden's heady mix of voluptuous flowers, jungly thickets of near-tropical growth, including palm trees, and complex rock and water formations bespeak an exotic ancestral mix, Amazonian rainforest providing half the genes, Alhambra garden stock the other half. The impact of this sinfully beautiful *mise-en-scène* can make an unsuspecting Mr and Mrs Smith feel like Adam and Eve exploring the world's first garden.

A strong sense of sequestration – emphasized by secret recesses and shadowed serpentine paths – was a deliberate aim from the outset. 'La Mortella should be experienced as a separate entity, a land beyond Ischia, both geographically and culturally,' explains Alessandra Vinciquerra, director of the Giardini La Mortella.

Centrepiece of the lower garden, the Fountain of the Four Pools was added by Russell Page in 1959 to his original design only once La Mortella could tap into Ischia's newly expanded water supply. Abundant calla lilies, strelitzia, Egyptian papyrus and water lilies would soon overrun the pond if not kept in check weekly by the garden staff.

Left: Another view of the Fountain of the Four Pools, with the wide leaves of the sacred or Indian lotus (*Nelumbo nucifera*) in the foreground and a wide variety of tree ferns in the back. Above centre: Many palm trunks wear a ruff of coleus. Above right: The Persian-style 'rill' Page used to connect the fountains in the garden's valley lent an exotic air and proved a highly useful irrigation conduit.

'The Waltons knew their inspiration must come from looking inward, not outward at the surrounding scene. Unlike other gardens in Campania, La Mortella doesn't flaunt its vistas of sea and sky as anyway, in most spots, thick canopies of trees prevent a visitor from seeing beyond the garden's borders. The Waltons wanted La Mortella to be a self-contained universe, a creative utopia.'

Entering the garden makes you feel, in fact, as if you have passed from one world to another. Your first sight is one of horticultural dazzle and enchantment: a stretch of garden that seems airlifted from the Court of Myrtles in the Generalife gardens of the Alahambra. Centred around a long stone rivulet, this lower 'valley' section of La Mortella unfolds like a tropical allée, where fountain jets spray calla lilies, strelitzia and Egyptian papyrus. Like a moist hand placed on a feverish cheek, this setpiece was designed by Page to take advantage of Ischia's then newly expanded water supply. Throughout the garden, indeed, the nearly musical susurration of water proved important to both Page and Walton.

From the Fountain of Four Pools, paths tempt the wanderer to explore lush and lavish thickets of *Magnolia* x *soulangeana*, *Calocedrus decurrens* and *Woodwardia radicans*. In hidden, overgrown nooks and crannies Page reveals his inspiration from the Islamic tradition of compartmentalized and successive garden 'rooms'. Their lavish foliage and amazing profusion of flowers is due to Page's dictum 'Don't plant one, plant a hundred': splendidly fertile, Ischia responded a hundredfold and, in places, La Mortella seems more a jungle than a garden.

Heading northwards, you pass *Jacaranda mimosifolia* – the first clue to the South American ambiance of the garden: the plant's homeland, Argentina, was shared by Lady Susana, who was instrumental in including many subtropical trees and plants at La Mortella. Looming ahead is the heart of the estate, the Fontana Grande. Here, in an egg-shaped pool, Page moved three gigantic volcanic boulders – he wrote that many were so artfully placed they must have been laid out 'by a Zen master in Kyoto' – and built a fountain into the largest in order to send up a spray of water over the pond. One stone path branches off to the Upper Garden and the Victoria House, a gorgeous greenhouse with an exotic backdrop – a enormous stone mask that is a homage to John Piper's set for Walton's *Façade* – that lends an magical air to orchids growing on tree trunks, tillandsias, bromeliads, a Borneo insect-eating *Nepenthes rajah*, and a pool where abound famously massive *Victoria amazonica* water lilies.

Threading over the precipitously steep hill surrounding the Fontana Grande are paths, paved with volcanic stone, that pass benches and sculpted sphinxes, and head ever upwards to the upper sections of the garden. 'There is a change in mood as you climb higher,' Signora Vinciquerra says. 'After Sir William's death in 1984, Lady Susana opened herself to the outside world by travelling to many countries as an ambassador for her husband's works. On her travels, she often brought back plants or seeds of rare species.' These include such exotica as dragon trees from the Canary Islands (*Dracaena draco*); the Chilean jasmine *Mandevilla laxa*; and the South African 'bird of paradise' tree (*Caesalpinia gilliesii*). Making friends in the Argentine embassy in Bangkok inspired Lady Susana to create a Thai garden, today planted with such species as *Philodendron erubescens* and presided over by a lovely teak pavilion.

La Mortella remains a very high-maintenance garden, not only because every other inch has a different plant (the garden is also the recipient of many donated horticultural collections) but because so many of the plants are unusual. 'We have seven gardeners, and some of them are highly specialized, as many blooms have different requirements. There is no such thing as a "typical" plant here at La Mortella!' says Signora Vinciquerra.

Near the crest of La Mortella, Lady Susana transformed an old water reservoir into the spectacular Temple of the Sun. Its three rooms are decorated with bas-reliefs of dramatic figures of Apollo and the Cumaean Sibyl, which loom over pools adorned with lilies

Above left: The Thai Garden, with its teak pavilion, was the result of one of Lady Walton's many 'pollinating' trips around the globe on behalf of her husband's musical legacy and foundation. Above centre: Among the many plants and flowers she shipped back from Thailand were these orange-tipped bromeliads. Right: The Cascata del Coccodrillo, or Crocodile Cascade, is a reward for those visitors intrepid enough to hike up to the highest reaches of the garden. A bench beneath of spreading *Chorisia speciosa* allows one to study the African blue lilies (*Agapanthus africanus*). On the far shore of the pond the plant looking like a dwarf palm with a tuft of big leaves is a rare encephalartos.

and creepers. Near the amphitheatre and recital hall – which both annually host a wide array of concerts sponsored by the Sir William Walton Trust (of which garden-lover HRH the Prince of Wales is chairman) – is the Crocodile Cascade, a popular photo-op, where sculpted crocodiles frolic over a cascade that flows into a pool adorned with *Nymphaea caerulea* from Egypt.

With something new to admire at nearly every step of the way, there is simply too much for horticulture fanciers to see for a visit to La Mortella to be truly relaxing. Fortunately, though, the terrace restaurant beckons. From here, one can savour the open-air canvas that is La Mortella and, with a glass of *vino bianco*, toast Lady Susana in thanks for the bevy of bewitchments that inspire all garden-lovers.

Top: Many varieties of water lilies festoon the garden ponds.
Above: Flanking the entry to the Victoria House are some of the
moisture-loving plants on show, including some crimson bromeliads
and pink *Phalaenopsis* orchids. Right: Framing the entrance to this
greenhouse are cascades of *Phalaenopsis* orchids, aerial tillandsias
and long beards of Spanish moss (*Tillandsia usneoides*) from the
south-eastern United States. In the water are *Victoria amazonica*,
the largest water lilies in the world.

It Has Been a Beautiful Day

Villa San Michele

Anacapri

The bus ride up to the Villa San Michele – set atop the Siren Heights of Anacapri 1,100 feet/300 metres above the Bay of Naples – is like a parachute drop in reverse. But just when you expect to hear, 'Next stop, pearly gates,' the carved oak doors of the villa appear and in a moment you are entering an oasis of beauty: a wondrously enticing cliffside garden that combines vestiges of formal classical design with the nineteenth-century romantic landscape tradition.

This extraordinary place was created by Axel Munthe, a Swedish physician who settled in Anacapri in the late nineteenth century, and whose subsequent philanthropic work on behalf of man, nature and animal earned him the sobriquet the 'angel of Anacapri'. His involvement with the island grew out of a case of love at first sight: while on a casual visit in 1876, he succumbed to its charms, found himself a cliffside perch, with an abandoned chapel, and returned ten years later to claim it for his own. He devoted the rest of his life, his imagination, his energies and his fortune to glorifying his beloved, and so succeeded that she became queen of Capri's houses. Dr Munthe was far from the first to succumb to Capri fever: back in the days of the ancient Roman Empire, even emperors became bewitched.

Though they were presumably engaged in monitoring the affairs of the Roman Empire, it is well known thatAugustus and Tiberius enjoying escaping here from overheated Rome. Augustus, who nicknamed the island Apragopolis ('the city of sweet idleness'), was primarily pleasure bound, while Tiberius used the privacy of his Villa Jovis on the Rocca de Capri – where he lived for the last ten years of his life, from AD 26 to 37 – to indulge in his most secret passion, the study of astronomy.

Travellers still arrive to enjoy innocent delights – sunning, sailing, fishing, scuba diving, romancing, wining, dining, inhaling, exhaling

A vibrant display of scarlet sage (*Salvia splendens*) draws all eyes to this view through the villa's re-creation of an ancient Roman *peristylium* arcade.

– and some never leave. Capri fever selects victims from any walk of life, from beachcomber to millionaire, though perhaps the latter can make the most of it. Friedrich Krupp, the founder of Germany's great munitions business, wired home to sell the factory. He wound up becoming a benefactor to half the island, bequeathing hospitals, the extraordinary Via Krupp and the estate that became the municipality's Gardens of Augustus, only to commit suicide when gossipmongers accused him of holding Roman-style orgies in secret Capri grottoes. Another northern European expat was Baron Jacques d'Adelsward-Fersen, a scion of immensely rich Lorraine industrialists, who built a shimmering white wedding cake called the Villa Lysis. But he too met an untimely end, choosing to end it all at the age of forty-two by taking a lethal dose of cocaine and champagne in the grotto pool of his magnificent house. Thanks to such scandals, by the early twentieth century it was felt, to quote the author John Gunther, that Capri was attracting 'the most fascinatingly debauched and corrupt set of Displaced Persons' ever known.

But if some of Capri's émigrés were considered devils, others were regarded as saints – in particular, Axel Munthe. His attachment to the island began during a casual stopover while on his Grand Tour – he was eighteen years old – when he unexpectedly came upon an abandoned chapel clinging to the hilly site of one of Emperor Tiberius's former palaces. Instantly taken with the beauty of the site, he vowed to return someday, never to leave. He went home to complete his studies and become a doctor, and was so successful that in a short time he had been named personal physician to the Swedish royal family, along with a panoply of other crowned heads. After ten years, his services having been handsomely compensated, he had accumulated sufficient wealth to honour his vow to return to Capri. But by then, the cholera epidemic of 1881–2 had broken out, and Dr Munthe selflessly stayed in Naples to minister to the impoverished citizens. After two years, in 1885 Munthe returned to Anacapri to practise medicine in the municipality. Once there, he quickly purchased the San Michele chapel site. In his 1929 book *The Story of San Michele*, he wrote: 'I am going to invent a style of my own, such that not even you shall be able to give it a name. No medieval twilight for me! I want my house open to sun and wind

Connecting the Chapel of San Michele with the main villa, the Friendship Walk – a path whose narrow width was designed to cajole visitors to walk along it as couples – is bordered by pairs of cypresses, which were lovingly transplanted as saplings from the Villa d'Este in Tivoli.

and the voice of the sea, like a Greek temple, and light, light, light everywhere!' He spent the years from 1889 to 1910 labouring to bring his vision to fruition.

'Light everywhere' being Munthe's chief requirement, the unclouded splendour of his chosen site was all that could be desired. The villa – his 'sanctuary to the sun' – is situated on one of Capri's highest points: the plateau of Anacapri, 1,000 feet/300 metres above the water on the flanks of Monte Barbarossa, which rises almost perpendicularly from the Bay of Naples. From this vertiginous height, the villa overlooks the Porta della Differencia gateway – built centuries ago to mark the border between the lower town of Capri and its arch-rival, Anacapri (Over Capri) – and sits atop the famous Scala Phoenica, a dizzying spiral of 777 stone steps constructed by ancient Greek colonizers of the island. It enjoys a catch-me-while-I-swoon vista of the entire Bay of Naples, with Naples off to the left, the Sorrentine peninsula to the right and Vesuvius front and centre.

Historians now know that the San Michele site was home to one of Capri's twelve imperial Roman residences. It was here, some think, far from the tiresome pomp and circumstance of empire, that Tiberius sought peace and solitude in his final years. Perhaps this last solace was denied him, as Dr Munthe reveals that he was told by some Caprioti that the bells of the Chapel of St Michael mysteriously rang at times – a sign that the emperor's damned soul had come back to ask forgiveness for having condemned a certain carpenter from Galilee to death.

Not for Dr Munthe those dark tales, however. He banished ghosts from his domain by creating a luxuriant and healing garden. His canvas was to be the vast flank of Monte Barbarossa, which stretched from the cliffside Via Porta up to the crumbling Crusader-era Castello Barbarossa. Unfortunately, by the nineteenth century the entire slope had been deforested (for the island's industries of shipbuilding, torches and fuel). However, following the 1904 publication of Norman Douglas's *Forestal Conditions of Capri*, the island's wealthy émigrés embarked on a reforestation programme, covering large tracts of land, primarily for the beautification of their new estates. Among these forest-saviours were the Cerio family at Monte Tragara; Lady Blanche Gordon-Lennox at Monte San Michele; Mario Astarita at Monte Tiberio; and Dr Axel Munthe at Monte Barbarossa. Their efforts transformed the once-barren flanks of mountain rock back into forest, with new growth of Aleppo pines, holm oaks, cypress hedges and many species of Mediterranean macchia.

In constructing his villa Dr Munthe began by making use of what already existed on the property: to the west, a house built in the simple style of a *casa di Capri*; to the east, a former gunpowder storehouse that had been converted into a chapel by the Protestant Count Nicholaus Papengouth. Neither would do in their present state. Munthe rebuilt the chapel, then expanded the simple main house and fitted it out with furnishings suitable for a villa. Then he put into place the masterstroke of his design: he linked the two now-improved structures with a pergola *all'antica* of thirty-seven columns of white Caprese stone. In breathtaking fashion, the regular spacing of its columns divided the vast panoramic vista of the Bay of Naples into discrete views, like so many framed pictures hanging on a wall. (Pergolas had also been one of the architectural leitmotifs of the Villa Jovis, the grandest of Emperor Tiberius's palaces, still visible across the island atop Monte Tiberio.) Aside from functioning as a view-framing device, Munthe's pergola – soon covered by thick vines and cypress branches – sheltered the garden from the winds that often blew across the Capodimonte cliffs of Anacapri. An enormous wind storm did in fact destroy the Great Pergola in 1959; the present one, cleverly designed to appear older than it is, dates back only to that year.

The initial inspiration for the estate was clearly the villas of the ancient Roman nobility, and you enter the garden area proper through a re-creation of a Roman *atrium*. With shimmering white walls, this small, balconied courtyard is studded with examples of the doctor's *roba di Tiberio* – antiquities excavated from the site, including a Corinthian column. A small arcaded loggia gives way to the main salons: the Venetian Salon, the master bedroom and the French Salon. These dim chambers, in turn, open up to the showpiece of the villa, the Sculpture Loggia, a grand re-creation of an ancient Roman *peristylium*, a four-sided, open-air vaulted arcade that surrounds a small garden courtyard. This is presided over by a copy of Verrocchio's *Boy on a Dolphin*, which prances amid a magnificent collection of palm trees, cytisus, and subtropical clumps of prickly pear, cacti and palmetto. Also known as the Cloister, the shady portico is decorated with Moorish-style tiles and crenellation

Dr Munthe monumentalized his passion for Capri's beauty by framing an incomparable vista of the Bay of Naples with a grand colonnade, a re-creation of a pergola *all'antica*, the kind Emperor Tiberius used to adorn his twelve island palaces. The thirty-seven columns of Caprese stone are today hung with wisteria.

and shelters the finest antique sculptures in Munthe's collection, including a bronze copy of the *Resting Mercury* (a famous sculpture excavated from Herculaneum in 1758), a gift from the city of Naples in thanks for his work in the cholera epidemic.

Just past the *Resting Mercury* is a platform from which steps lead to the pergola and main garden, where a magnificent array of bedding plants and other flowers compete with the sea vistas visible all along the walk. Tall trees thrust high above the colourful plantings. In addition to indigenous species, Munthe imported rare tree specimens from Japan and Australia, which are still thriving and, like the many sculptures, add variety and lend a touch of otherworldliness to the scene. Honouring his Nordic roots, Dr Munthe planted a stand of white birch, but after sulking for a while the saplings died. Years later the villa's first curator, Josef Oliv, discovered, through experimentation, that birch trees could thrive here if kept refrigerated for their first three years and only then transplanted. Now their fallen leaves provide an annual autumnal spectacle.

Among the most striking trees on the estate are the soaring, dark-green cypresses, often used in cemeteries and long seen in legend and mythology as symbols of death and resurrection. As one of the groundbreaking adherents of hypnosis in psychological practice, Munthe was intensely interested in the connection between Hypnos, the ancient Greek god of sleep, and his twin brother Thanatos, the god of death.

As his use of cypress trees demonstrates, Munthe proved as much an artistic as a horticultural classicist: the main plants in the garden are ones immortalized in many ancient works of art, such as ilex and laurel, and *Acanthus* species, whose leaves decorate so many carved friezes, Corinthian capitals and crown mouldings in Roman architecture. While the bones of his garden were evergreen trees and plants, Munthe also wanted to spice things up with some seasonal glories, and thus planted camellias, flowering ash, azaleas, Chinese wisteria, hydrangeas, roses, agapanthus, busy Lizzies – choices perhaps influenced by the Art Nouveau movement, all the rage in the decorative arts of the early twentieth century – plus indigenous wild flowers such as myrtle, broom, rock rose and others. Ilsa Girgonsone, botanical curator of the Villa San Michele, notes, 'Attested to by the magnificent bouquets – arranged in antique pots, neo-classical amphoras and *objets d'art* vases – that adorned the doctor's salons is the fact that he loved flowers,' and adds, 'The annual calendar at the villa is marked by dazzling colours, spring arriving with hyacinths and tulips, then the camellia trees bursting into bloom at the end of April; June and July bring cineraria and impatiens in many hues.'

The price of manmade beauty is often faithful attendance to its upkeep, and it became clear to Dr Munthe that the most pressing need for the survival of his beloved creation was a plentiful supply of water. This was achieved by the installation of huge cisterns on the Barbarossa hillside, whereby nutrient-rich run-off from the mountain could be collected and directed to the plantings. By this method he succeeded in keeping the thirsty garden blooming year round, becoming one of the first on Capri to divert water to a garden with purely ornamental value. 'The flowers benefited also from the villa's northern exposure,' Signora Girgonsone remarks, 'which created an invigorating microclimate: even on the hottest days, the *Rosa banksia*, *Wisteria sinensis* and hydrangea are pampered by caressing breezes.'

To the right of the Grand Pergola are steps to a shady and secluded enfilade of *giardinetti* – little garden rooms carpeted with

fine green lawns and beds of bright peonies, and linked by a winding stone path. At the far end of the pergola a curved belvedere allows visitors to view the entirety of Capri and the Bay of Naples – a heavenly vista. From here, a tiny spiral of steps leads upwards to the Chapel of San Michele, which sits upon a slate terrace presided over by an Etruscan sphinx. To the chapel's left, overlooking the bay, a loggia lined with 'medievalized' triple-sash, Norman-arched trifore windows houses the famous Egyptian sphinx, a 3,200-year-old sculpture. You cannot see its face – intentionally – but legend says that any wish made while stroking its left hind leg with the left hand will come true. Some wishes come true years after they are made, so who is to say?

The chapel leads to the Cypress Walk, which guides you down a gently sloping hill. Dr Munthe called this the Friendship Walk, because the paired rows of trees – the saplings came from the

Opposite: Decorated with Moorish-style tilework and home to a copy of Verrocchio's *Boy on a Dolphin*, the cloister is also shaded by a lovely collection of palm trees, cytisus and subtropical clumps of prickly pear, cacti and palmetto. Above: A grand recreation of an ancient Roman *peristylium*, the Sculpture Gallery is home to the finest works in Dr Munthe's collection, including this bronze copy of the *Resting Mercury* (the original resides in Naples's world-famous archaeological museum), bestowed on the doctor by the city in honour of his work combating cholera in its streets.

Above left: Peopled throughout with marbles and bronzes of Greek gods and
Roman emperors, the villa is like a three-dimensional Alma-Tadema painting.
Above right: Dark tales clung to this place, once the site of one of Emperor
Tiberius's Caprese villas. Local legend had it that the ringing of bells from the
villa chapel was a sign that the spirit of Tiberius was begging forgiveness for
sentencing a certain carpenter from Galilee. Munthe banished the shadows,
making his villa the queen of Capri's gardens.

gardens of the Villa d'Este, in Tivoli – lined the path so closely that visitors were forced to walk as couples. This charming and evocative promenade – bordered by a burbling brook constructed by Dr Munthe – leads back to the villa.

Once Dr Munthe's master vision had been fulfilled, his villa provided not only comfort but also an endless spectacle for his guests. Reflecting the aesthetic flavour of a Alma-Tadema painting, the house is a fantasia of parapets, colonnaded arbours, loggias, arcades, and Greek porticoes, peopled throughout with marbles and bronzes of Greek gods and Roman emperors. Grafted on to this are elements of romantic medievalism – the Romanesque trifore windows, gilded Gothic statues of the Madonna and fifteenth-century wooden church stalls. And, enough apparently never being enough so long as more exotica could be found, to these Munthe added objects made fashionable by the nineteenth-century passion for things Moroccan, Egyptian and Spanish. By installing an array of props – which included Romanesque mosaics and Renaissance

Above left: Studded with examples of *roba di Tiberio* – antiquities excavated from the site by Munthe – this Roman-style atrium is the entryway to the main enfilade of salons in the house. Above centre: A view from the *peristylium* shows how beautifully the villa coupled interior shelter with exterior light. Right: Lining the Friendship Walk are some exotic species, such as this English leopard plant (*Senecio kaempferi*).

reliquaries – he created a kind of *wunderkammer* and transformed the main salons into virtual stagesets. Pride of place in these was given to the *roba di Tiberio* – the antiquities which had been excavated from the site. Some of his acquisitions were of dubious provenance: J. Pierpont Morgan appeared at the villa one night intent on purchasing the jewel of the collection, the Oracle of Phidias – a gigantic stone mask said to have been carved by the greatest ancient Greek sculptor – and was none the wiser when his million-dollar offer was refused; only Munthe knew the mask was a forgery. In

the end, the Villa San Michele became a veritable potpourri of styles. Henry James had the last word, describing the villa as 'the most fantastic beauty, poetry, and inutility that one had ever seen clustered together'.

Not very well known is the fact that Dr Munthe, in addition to his other credentials, was a pioneer in the field of neurology. He treated some of the most aristocratic people on earth for 'nervous conditions'. Among the crowned heads who arrived on Capri to pay a call were the Empress Eugenie, wife of Napoleon III; the Tsarina Alix of Russia (whose family was building a villa across the bay, in Sorrento); Queen Victoria of Sweden, who it is said became the doctor's soulmate and – according to some – his *amour*; and Austria's Empress Elizabeth, the famous 'Sissi' of the Habsburgs.

Dr Munthe's most exasperating visitor was not a client but a full-time guest, the Marchesa Casati, the fabulous fin-de-siècle creature who dazzled Paris by walking down the Champs-Elysées with a jewel-collared panther. Immensely rich, she had already transformed Paris's Palais Rose and Venice's Palazzo dei Leoni into extravagant showcases for her costume balls and literary get-togethers. Painted by Boldini, John and Van Dongen, dressed by Poiret, photographed by Man Ray and Cecil Beaton, and muse to the Italian Futurists, she descended on Capri and bullied her way into a lease of the Villa San Michele. She proved to be the only person who actually lived there (the good doctor resided at the guesthouse on the property at the time) and her summer tenancies were so fraught with drama and lawsuits (her rent was often in arrears) that Munthe never hired the villa out again. She also felt that the garden left something to be desired and before long had adorned the grounds with floridly coloured Venetian glass blooms (created specially for her in Murano). Her garden parties, at which guests were shadowed by an enormous paper moon that moved across the grounds by pulley, became the talk of the island.

Just as the good doctor ministered to people, so he helped animals. *The Story of San Michele* describes his miniature baboon named Billy, whose unsupervised bouts with beer and whisky caused chaos all over the island. Munthe also befriended a tiny owl whose wings were broken; it never left the doctor's side and gazed at him adoringly at all times. When the local quail population was threatened with wholesale destruction, because the Anacapresi had discovered that the pitiful song of a blinded quail brought many other birds to its aid, making them easy targets for hunters, our latter-day St Francis sold a quantity of his personal treasures and used the funds to purchase the entire Barbarossa hillside, making it off limits to hunters and

protecting the quails' nesting grounds. The hill is still maintained as a wildlife sanctuary.

Sadly, Munthe lost the use of his left eye to glaucoma in 1910. The man who had once sought 'light, light everywhere' could only venture out at night, so as to avoid the harsh sunlight. Seeking shade, he purchased the Torre di Materita, which was just up the hill from the Villa San Michele.

The saintly doctor's last years on Capri were spent in this shadowy, medieval tower and so perhaps it is only fitting to conclude with one of his poignant passages from *The Story of San Michele*: 'It is good to wander about in the soft light under the olives of Materita. It is good to sit and dream in the old tower, it is about the only thing I can do now. The tower looks towards the West, where the sun sets. Soon the sun will sink into the sea, then comes the twilight, then comes the night. It has been a beautiful day.'

Left and above: The end of the Grand Pergola leads to a tiny corkscrew stairway that ascends to the Chapel of San Michele and the Sphinx Terrace, home to the famous Egyptian sphinx. Enjoying a vista that crowns the island's Siren Heights, the creature resides in its own belvedere. Visitors cannot see the creature's head – intentionally – but if they stroke its hind legs with their left hand and hope for their heart's desire, rumour has it that their wish will come true.

The Island Way

La Certosella

Capri

When the rich, fashionable and highly cultivated arrived in Capri en masse at the end of the nineteenth century, they quickly made the island into a millionaire's playpen. Transforming it through glamour and money into a destination for pleasure and holidaymaking, the new arrivals set out to build extravagantly beautiful villas. These included Lady Blanche Gordon-Lennox's Palladian palace, the Villa Monte San Michele; Baron Jacques d'Adelsward-Fersen's D'Annunzio-esque, Belle-Epoque temple, the Villa Lysis; and the Wolcott-Perry sisters' fantastic neo-Moorish Villa Torricella. Once building was completed, the owners turned their attention to the grounds, and soon everyone was vying with their neighbour to create the most beautiful landscaped spot in the universe.

Masterminding some of these horticultural extravaganzas was a Neapolitan gardener named Mimi Ruggiero. Like his patrons, Ruggiero inclined towards botanical snobbery. Under his supervision, Baron Fersen's mansion became enshrined in seas of fuchsia, hortensia, azaleas, geranium and jasmine. Ruggiero's lavish plan called for wisteria and iris to bloom in the spring; solanum to appear in the height of summer; and plumbago and belladonna lilies to close the season. The downside to this floriferous symphony was the cost, as most of the plants chosen by Ruggiero – which incidentally were supplied by Ruggiero's own nursery, conveniently located on the island – were 'florist' or exotic rather than indigenous varieties. Critics began to wail that the super-cultivated varieties tended to have flowers so repetitively perfect they appeared artificial.

In their defence against this new style of gardening, Capri's old-fashioned *giardini* had their own staunch champion, Edwin Cerio, one-time mayor of the island (1920–23), whose greatest passion was to keep Capri's horticulture free from foreign species. As a botanist, he had laid out some of Capri's most venerable – and venerated – gardens. He had also designed fashionable *stile Caprese* villas, including the Villa Il Rosaio. Encyclopedic knowledge of Caprese flora and fauna made him the leading conservationist of the island's native species and in 1922 he hosted a widely publicized Conference for the Defense of Capri's Landscape, at which he addressed such controversial topics as invasive tourism, wilderness management and deforestation – decades before these subjects became hotly debated issues.

To his mind, the plant racketeers who were importing hundreds of bougainvillea and gigantic palm trees to Capri were bastardizing Capri's natural landscape and displacing native species by becoming invasive. Like the Saracen pirates of the seventeenth century, the new rich had arrived to pillage and sack the island. One of his many books, *Guida Inutile di Capri*, was a guidebook explicitly written to keep people from visiting by drawing attention to all the island's faults and foibles, such as warning (incorrectly) that the island's flora was mainly comprised of '*piante velenose*' (poisonous plants). More to the point, his book *Flora Privata di Capri* threw down the gauntlet by stating 'the Caprese garden has to remain Caprese'. Or to quote Amedeo Maiuri's introduction to the book: 'Those who have defended Capri against literary exotica now defend the island against floral exotica. Perverting species, propagating the most unnatural hybrids, introducing exotic, insidious and invasive plants in the name of servile appeasement to the vulgar taste for international tourist-class flora, is tantamount to culpability for the incitement to criminal behaviour; one commits the gravest possible crime against the divine and primordial beauty of the island's landscape.'

Vowing to save what native plants he could (author Bruno Manfellotto described the role of Capri as that of a botanical Noah's Ark), Cerio declared open warfare against this '*scandalo vegetale*'. He vigorously attacked, for instance, any new plantings of *Echium fastuosum*, a towering bush with enormous blue blossoms that Lady

Originally built in 1880 for Camille du Locle, director of Paris's Opéra Comique and librettist of Verdi's *Aida* and *La Forza del Destino*, La Certosella was redesigned in quintessential Caprese style by Edwin Cerio, the island's leading designer of villas and gardens.

Gordon-Lennox's Scottish gardeners had introduced to the island. Its spread over sections of the island was so rampant – especially in the Località Faraglioni – that Cerio dubbed it *Echium infestuosum* (infesting), and in his *Flora Privata* wrote that he wished a plague of parasites would finish it off, along with all other foreign species taking root. As it turns out, the gardens he designed to epitomize the historic *stile di Capri* were another of his 'weapons'.

One of the most spectacular examples was at the Villa La Certosella, part of the vast Cerio estate. Resting at the foot of Monte Tuoro, the estate flanked sizeable stretches of Via Tragara – described by some admirers 'the most beautiful street in the world' – and comprised several of the island's most notable houses, including Villa Tragara, Villa Quattrocolonne and Villa Ada, all occupied by members of the island's growing literary and artistic colony. Built in 1880 by the head of Paris's Opéra Comique, Camille du Locle (librettist of Verdi's *Aida*, *Don Carlo* and *La Forza del Destino*), La Certosella had been enlarged into a grand edifice by Jan Styka, illustrator of Sienkiewicz's *Quo Vadis?*, with additions that included Italian Renaissance-style ornamentation and stone caryatids, and featured a gigantic columned temple to Apollo as the centrepiece of the garden. In keeping with his enduring 'Caprese first' sentiments, Edwin requisitioned the house back into the Cerio estate and, by

totally dismantling the Renaissance decor, returned La Certosella to its roots as a *casa mediterranea*.

He began the process by replacing the ornate Corinthian columns of the Tempio di Apollo with a *colonnato di casa contadina* – a pergola constructed of columns in the simple Doric style, each topped by a capital of Sorrentine grey tufa. Pergolas were a main component of Cerio's return to a *Capri antica* style, as well as being symbolic stand-ins for the oak or chestnut poles formerly used to support the grape vines and climbing creepers that once abounded on Capri. Such pergolas were traditionally used to expand the parameters of a house; over time, their double columns, finished in white plaster, were adopted as permanent solutions to a seasonal farming need. Forming a giant arbour, Cerio's square *pergola rustica* at La Certosella echoes the outline of the garden's main parterre. Below the network of grape vines that encircle the pergola's columns – forming, according to Cerio, 'a decoration that man's ornate plasterwork can never equal' – he planted crocus, gladiolus, daffodils, asphodel, violets, oleander, hortensia, amemones and bellflowers – all unimpeachably Caprese species.

As it happens, the winds of change did ultimately flutter the leaves at La Certosella and the garden today is home to many of the plants Edwin Cerio once prohibited. Clouds of mimosa (native to Queensland and Tasmania) colour the sky yellow through the winter months; the famed 'Regina della Notte' (Queen of the Night), which keeps sleep-deprived gardeners on the alert until the one night of the year when it blooms, is one of several exotic cactus species on view; groups of antique olive-oil urns overflow with red geraniums and pink primroses; bougainvilleas of infinite variety dangle over porticos; the orange of strelitzia burns brightly from October through June; 'Gelsomino' jasmine adds its heady perfume to the air; and particoloured hibiscus plantings line paths beneath the villa's balconies.

The magnificent gardens at La Certosella are kept growing and thriving by the tender care of owners Signora Ilaria Iacona and her mother, Angela, who, since 1959, have made La Certosella one of Capri's most beloved hotels. With the help of a single gardener –

Opposite: La Certosella's porch, home to magnificent succulents such as this euphorbia, is shaded by a canopy of bougainvillea. Left: Cerio replaced du Locle's neo-Renaissance stone pergolas and statues of gods with a *pergola rustica* of the kind first used by island farmers, who borrowed its simple Doric style from ancient Roman settlers.

quite an amazing feat when you consider the results of their labours – they have babied the estate's flowering lemon, orange and grapefruit trees, whose yields are turned into fresh juices and homemade jams that are served to delighted hotel guests.

Visitors to Capri who come with hopes of finding *stile di Capri* gardens are thrilled when they discover (hidden as it is above a stone staircase) the real thing. While La Certosella's 'Caprisità' (Capri-ness) is no longer strictly as pure as in the past, it nevertheless remains the best example of a vernacular garden on this beauteous island.

Above left: Harking back to regional garden styles centuries old, La Certosella's porch is, in fact, a careful re-creation devised by Edwin Cerio in the early twentieth century. Above centre: Roses are not rare on Capri but most flower and die before the midsummer heat arrives. Right: Once the prime source of water, this Gothic well head sits at the centre of the garden and makes a picturesque setting for myriad plants, including roses, euphorbia and red hibiscus in pots.

III

SIREN-LAND

Sorrento &
the Sorrentine Peninsula

How Does Lord Astor's Garden Grow?

Villa Tritone

Sorrento

Given the loveliness and repose of its Old World setting on the Bay of Naples, it was inevitable that the surging tide of American millionairedom of the early twentieth century should break upon the shores of Sorrento. As Vanderbilts and Mellons arrived they found themselves in excellent company, past and present: emperors, poets, celebrities of every ilk, European nobles and legions of mere mortals have all succumbed to the seductive spell of Surrentum – 'Land of the Sirens'. The three *sirene* of the Odysseus legend, Parthenope, Leucosia and Ligeia, whose song so tempted Homer's hero, made their home in these waters, and one look at Sorrento's dreamy coastal promontory tells you why they came so close to ensnaring Odysseus.

Fast-forward several millennia to 1904, when another traveller arrived and found the sirens' song to his liking. He was none other than William Waldorf Astor, 'the landlord of New York' and the richest man in America. On a trip to Rome, he had travelled south to Sorrento and come upon a priceless stretch of real estate: the cliffside villa once owned by Agrippa Posthumus, grandson to the great Augustus, founder of the ancient Roman empire. What better place for a twentieth-century emperor like Astor to put down roots?

Like Edith Wharton, John Singer Sargent, Bernard Berenson and other American expats, the 1st Viscount Astor (he received his title from George V in gratitude for the millions he had bestowed on charities) had become a person who had perfected 'the art of not going home'. It was as if he had stepped out of the pages of Henry James's *The Ambassadors* when, in 1882, he reached his first pinnacle of prestige and President Chester Arthur appointed him American Minister to Italy. At that time, to be an American in Italy was the most fashionable thing. Poverty was stalking the noblest families of Rome and the Astor millions quickly made him the new proprietor of the spectacular Palazzo Pallavincini-Rospigliosi in Rome. While he was a failure as a diplomat – his pathologically shy temperament thwarted the camaraderie needed in diplomatic circles – he found his true calling as a collector of art, especially the ancient antiquities then so temptingly for sale in Rome.

By 1891, Astor had lost his bid for a US senate seat and, worse, his wife had lost her title as society's supreme social arbiter – a sceptre stubbornly grasped by his aunt, Caroline Astor, 'the' Mrs Astor. Smarting from these insults and also smitten with Europe's *allures de noblesse*, Astor moved his family to a land better suited to the pastimes of a billionaire: England. Bidding America adieu, this man of fastidious taste set about establishing roots in his adopted land, and England's stately homes beckoned.

In 1893 Astor acquired Cliveden in Buckinghamshire, a grand example of the stately home, which he filled with Louis XV bibelots, Roman sarcophagi and Venetian ceilings. In 1903, he bought Hever Castle in Kent, haunted family seat of Anne Boleyn, to which he added a 'Tudor village' and vast gardens. During this period, he tried his hand at the kind of pursuits to be expected of an over-achiever with unlimited resources and, in quick succession, bought several British newspapers, acquired racehorses, founded a literary journal and took a crack at writing – two novels set during the Italian Renaissance. Eventually, he focused his greatest energies on a field much more to his liking, art, and amassed a collection that would have impressed Lorenzo de' Medici. And when he travelled down to Sorrento and came upon the Villa Tritone, he found the perfect place to showcase his collection of ancient Roman antiquities.

A favourite of Sorrento's transplanted English owners, *Rosa banksiae*, a climbing rose species, was often used to frame views of the Bay of Naples.

Above: The southern terrace of the estate overlooks Sorrento's Marina Grande and is home to a rock garden planted with such cacti as this *Agave americana*. Right: Set on a towering bluff, the villa was first owned by Count Labonia as a repository for his archaeological collection and then enlarged and rebuilt when Lord William Waldorf Astor took over the estate.

Perched high on a bluff of tufa, Sorrento overlooks a panorama that is magnificent in its sweep: the entire natural arena of the Bay of Naples, from bella Napoli, on the left, to Mount Vesuvius on the right, whose looming presence gives the landscape a sudden, theatrical intensity. Just to the north lies the superlatively fertile Piano di Sorrento, a large plain where the *masserie* (farms) are famed for their fruitfulness; this is a region where the soft warm air is redolent of the penetrating fragrance of orange blossom and where there are the most famous lemon tree groves in Italy. Just to the south lies the natural amphitheatre created by the Lattari mountains, whose sheltering peaks give Sorrento its greenhouse coddling. Here, winter is only a word.

Even in ancient times, the town was the darling of tourism. Both Ovid and Virgil often escaped to its balmy clime from Rome, a city overheated at times by more than scorching weather. Virgil – author of the *Aeneid* and the *Georgics*, poetic paeans to the tranquil delights of rural Campania – gave the thumbs up to Surrentum for *otium* (leisure), thumbs down for *negotium* (business). The perfect place for lotus-eating, the town easily lured the superstars of the Grand Tour era, such as Lord Byron, the Duke of Wellington, Sir Walter Scott,

and Goethe. Verdi, Dumas *père* and Oscar Wilde headed here – for inspiration, perhaps? Likewise emperors and kings – to escape the madding crowd, or their mistresses?

The Villa Tritone was owned by one of Lord Astor's collecting competitors, Count Giovanni Labonia. Then named Aux Roches Grises – an allusion to the towering bluff on which it sits – the villa nestled within a vast garden laid out by the count. At its centre were the ruins of a monastery destroyed by Saracen pirates; at the end of the sixteenth century, Dominican monks had rebuilt it as the Convento di San Vincenzo and it found fame as a retreat for the poet Torquato Tasso (whose family home was on adjacent property). Here the friars grew the first citrus trees imported from the Middle East, whose legacy was the immense lemon and orange groves that

Left: Some scholars see Lord Astor's stone wall pierced by apertures – here a Roman bifore window softened by a frame of variegated ivy – as influenced by the rules of *shakkei*, or 'borrowed landscape', in Japanese aesthetics, fashionable during the Edwardian era. Below: When Lord William Waldorf Astor proceeded to wall in his estate's most spectacular vista of the Bay of Naples, critics called him 'Walled-off Astor', but the need for a barrier against the sea winds, not privacy, was the main reason the wall was built. The white flowers of *Yucca elephantipes* and different species of agave accent this section of the garden, while wisteria, below, climbs happily over this part of the stone wall.

continued to enrich the Sorrentine economy for centuries. After Astor purchased the estate in 1905, he promptly began to restore it.

Like a remnant from an ancient golden age, which of course it is, the villa sits on a curved clifftop high above the Bay of Naples. Heinrich Schliemann, the father of archaeology and discoverer of ancient Troy, called the view of Vesuvius from this perch the best in the land, and Sorrento's charms are nowhere greater than in the gardens of the Villa Tritone (named for a sixth-century BC sculpted metope of a Triton mounted on the sea wall of the estate). Today it is the domain of Mariano and Rita Pane, whose careful and reverent hands have restored the estate to its full Astor-esque splendour.

The garden is an extraordinary mixture of English and Italian styles, where Picturesque and Gothic Revival notes have been introduced over a classic substratum, making it a supreme example of – and monument to – a style that might be called English Exoticism. Visitors are invariably struck by the sheer abundance of trees and plants, which, interlaced with lush vines, palms and yuccas, give the impression of carefree disorder. Bursts of colourful flowers – including fuchsias, orange clivia and agapanthus – accent the cypress-lined avenues and shaded allées. In sections, large patches are encouraged to reveal nature 'left to itself', while other areas adhere to the more formal dictates of the Italian garden, in which artful effects are achieved by planting and tweaking every flower to look just so.

And there is so much green! 'Greens are the most amiable of colours,' remarks Signora Pane, the garden's benefactor and author of *I Giardino* (2002, Rizzoli) and *I Sapori del Sud*, a cookery book of southern Italian recipes. The signora is beloved by horticultural societies around the world, as she not only tends the estate but often personally leads tours through it for other interested green-thumbed folk. 'How friendly green is to other colours, no?' she points out, adding, 'It is the coolest of colours – it rests the eye and lifts the spirit. On stressful days, I find being in this garden as soothing as an herbal eye-mask!'

Signora Pane knows every plant species in the garden as well as a mother knows her children. As she tours the garden, one learns that Astor imported many floricultural treasures from distant lands: beaucarnea from Mexico, cycas from Polynesia and Australia, erythrina from Brazil, *Strelitzia nicolai* from South Africa, chamaedorea from Nicaragua, jacaranda from Chile, araucaria from Patagonia and jubaea from Egypt. As it happens, Astor was in a continual neck-and-neck race for rare and exotic species with Princess Cortchacow, a member of the imperial Russian family, who was just as passionate about developing her own grand villa garden in the St Agnello suburb across town (now the Parco dei Principi).

As the layout of the garden unfolds, it reveals its treasures in a series of delightful surprises. The interplay of dense growths – cyathea, asplenium, nephrolepis, *Woodwardia radicans* ferns – creates a hide-and-seek setting, leading you moment by moment from shadowy wilderness to an open sunlit space, where you might be confronted by a medieval statue of a saint standing sentinel or a belvedere overlooking the Bay of Naples. Following in Count Labonia's footsteps, Astor viewed the garden as a *passeggiata archeologica* (archaeological promenade), and indeed, the garden's rich verdancy provides a sympathetic surrounding for the sculptures he installed in it.

The pageant of statuary begins with a likeness of Neptune from eighteenth-century Florence, which, set in a grove of yuccas, presides over the sunken garden parterre laid out directly in front of the villa. This figure alludes to the fact that Agrippa Posthumus was an enthusiastic fisherman – the ancient stone pools where he farmed moray eels can still be spotted just below the villa at the water's edge – and liked to call himself Neptune. With a design attributed to Giambologna, the lifesize sculpture stands by a small lily pond that anchors one end of the parterre. The parterre comprises eight beds of silvery lavender and lantana, and it is framed by marble vases of white pelargoniums and walls covered with rambling white roses.

Beckoning you onwards is an ancient sculpture of a siren, given pride of place in a medieval trifore window overlooking the bay. This figure is the opening salvo in the garden's most extraordinary setpiece: a 10-foot/3-metre-high stone wall along the garden's edge which closes off the panorama of the bay except for three narrow openings that allow only limited glimpses of the precious view: the trifore window, a Roman bifore window and a parapet-enclosed marble terrace. Audacious as ever, Astor whimsically divided one of the most sought-after panoramas in all Italy into three scenic 'quotations', using these openings as framing devices. Some scholars

have tentatively attributed this conceit to the Aesthetic movement's interest in Far Eastern motifs; others say, 'Hmm, maybe.' But at about the same time, along with fashionable fin-de-siècle London, whose tastes were constantly changing, Astor discovered the charms of Japanese art, and one of its techniques, called *shakkei*, or 'borrowed landscape', allowed the gardener to use a distant feature outside the garden such as a mountain or grove of ancient trees as an element of the garden, with plantings completing the composition. Closer to home, the vogue for *vedutismo* – the nineteenth-century Italian landscape painting school of picturesque vistas – may have also influenced Astor to create these three 'paintings' of the bay.

There is another, much more prosaic explanation. Prizing his privacy, the reclusive financier had already stirred up a hornet's nest of bad publicity by walling in his Cliveden and Hever Castle estates (defacing, in the process, famously scenic stretches of the English countryside). William Waldorf Astor had thus earned himself the nickname of 'Walled-off Astor' in newspapers and journals. But whether it was built for privacy, or the genuine need to protect his villa from fierce winds blowing off the bay, the sea-gazing wall allows the visitor to enjoy some serious Bay of Naples voyeurism.

Running parallel to the wall is an allée pleasantly shaded by a riot of *Elaeagnus pungens* and yellow Banksia roses. This allée leads to a long marble balustrade, fully open to sun and sea, on which sit, in a magisterial line-up, the sculpted heads of the Roman gods Mercury, Dionysius, Jupiter, Juno and Mars, each on his own pedestal. Their august expressions lend the accumulated gravity of centuries to the scene, but ancient they are not: they were created for Astor by Sir Lawrence Alma-Tadema, the Victorian painter whose minutely detailed paintings of Roman marbles, mosaics and maidens were dubbed 'marbellous' by *Punch*. Astor had met Alma-Tadema at one of the artist's Monday afternoon 'at homes', at his house in St John's Wood, London, said by many to be a veritable Pompeiian palace – a description that would have been irresistible to Astor.

Right: A Roman bifore window frames a classic view of Vesuvius. Overleaf, left: The brightest spot of colour in the garden is lent by the firecracker-red leaves of an *Erythrina christa-galli*. Overleaf, right: At one end of this allée – flanked by palm trees in terracotta pots, bordered by orange *Tritonia crocata* and covered with a chestnut trellis of white Banksia roses – is a fountain from Lord Astor's sculpture collection.

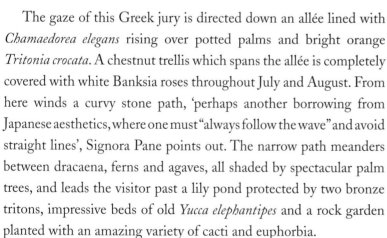

The gaze of this Greek jury is directed down an allée lined with *Chamaedorea elegans* rising over potted palms and bright orange *Tritonia crocata*. A chestnut trellis which spans the allée is completely covered with white Banksia roses throughout July and August. From here winds a curvy stone path, 'perhaps another borrowing from Japanese aesthetics, where one must "always follow the wave" and avoid straight lines', Signora Pane points out. The narrow path meanders between dracaena, ferns and agaves, all shaded by spectacular palm trees, and leads the visitor past a lily pond protected by two bronze tritons, impressive beds of old *Yucca elephantipes* and a rock garden planted with an amazing variety of cacti and euphorbia.

Not far from a Gothic well head – the only remnant of the medieval monastery that once stood here – is the signora's favourite tree: an *Erythrina christa-galli* which, when it is covered in bright red leaves in May and June, she calls 'a horticultural firecracker'. Beyond this spot is a Gothic-style gate set in a wall with niches that harbour various medieval and antique sculptures, including a St John and a Madonna and Child. The pathway then leads to the eastern sector of the garden, where an alcove worked in antique *opus reticulatum*

Opposite: The main entrance road is lined with exotic palm species, including Canary palms (*Phoenix canariensis*) and Mediterranean fan palms (*Chamaerops humilis*). Above left: Small succulents grow in the South Terrace's rock garden, along with the big ball-shaped cacti known as golden barrel (*Echinocactus grusonii*). Above right: Set in a grove of yucca and palms, this copy of Giambologna's *Neptune* lords it over a lily pond and a parterre planted with silvery-leaved lavender.

Laid out as a *passeggiata archeologica* (archaeological promenade), the main garden path begins at the Belvedere of the Siren, left, and ends on the Western Terrace right, with ever-present Vesuvius stage front and centre.

is the setting for an early Christian sarcophagus of an unidentified man and woman. An enormous statue of Juno presides over this area, reminding us not only that Astor had distanced himself from Edwardian opulence (in 1905, he had bestowed his Cliveden estate in England on his son, Waldorf, on the occasion of his wedding to Miss Langhorne who, as Nancy Astor, became the new social leader of the family) but that he leaned particularly towards Roman monumentality.

Willy Astor returned to England only towards the latter part of his life, perhaps to be closer to his new amour, Lady Victoria Sackville-West (mother of Vita). From 1905 to about 1915, Sorrento was his Shangri-La, and he continued to improve it. During those years the ruins of the medieval convent were demolished and in its place he erected a marble terrace, beside whose grandiosity those in ancient Athens and DeMille's movies were said to pale. The terrace became the site of the Villa Pompeiana, Astor's recreation of the House of the Vettii, a residence uncovered in the excavations of Pompeii. This pleasure pavilion would have delighted Alma-Tadema, had he seen it. Inside, its salons glow with panels Astor had painted in sunset colours and walls alive with nymphs and sea creatures in the Pompeiian style of the second century AD. The villa is now part of the Hotel Bellevue-Syrene, whose elegance made it a favourite of such guests as Empress Eugenie of France and Ludwig I of Bavaria. Historians may say the villa of Agrippa Posthumus disappeared long ago, but to see the pavilion that William Waldorf Astor created in homage to that age makes one ask 'Really?'

Today, the flowers of the Villa Tritone's garden seem to smile whenever Signora Pane walks by, especially when she can close her gates and enjoy traipsing barefoot along the mossy terrace overlooking Sorrento's Marina Grande (at the southern end of the estate). The mosses remain verdant even into the winter months, supporting her view that there is no one right time to view this garden. 'Every morning I find a new "best" somewhere in the garden,' she says with a knowing and loving smile.

Song of the Sirens
Li Galli
off Positano

Nature was the first artist, and since time began her hand has been continually sculpting the work of art that is the Sorrentine peninsula. The promontory's many gnarled pinnacles, crescent coves and towering cliffs prove the force of her creative powers again and again. Here, in the Bocce di Capri, the bay that separates two of the most beautiful gulfs in the world, she saw fit to hurl three rocky dots into the sea: Li Galli. These islands seem to fit together like geological jigsaw pieces or the components of a Henry Moore sculpture. Though tiny in size, they are giants in the realm of legend. In the *Odyssey,* Homer tells us that Parthenope, Leucosia and Ligeia, three waterborne sirens – legendary sea creatures, half-fish, half-woman – sang an intoxicating song here that lured many a seafarer to his death. The only person to escape was the wily navigator Odysseus, who had himself tied to his ship's mast and sealed the ears of his crew with wax. The Sirens slew themselves in frustration, leaping from the nearby Sorrentine mainland and turning into the three islets.

Today, you alight from your boat to find an aborginal beach club – primeval rocks, a sandy shore littered with shards of classical amphorae and an ancient Roman anchorage. But the sight of youthful goddesses – displaying bikini-clad contours the equal of ancient statues – diving into the sea from a nearby yacht brings you right back to the present. We are, indeed, far from days when those three pithecanthropic pretties slew themselves in frustration. Centuries later, these Sirens not only offer a powerful story but are an indelible symbol for travellers who chose to expatriate themselves to a new homeland.

One such, in the twentieth century, was Ballets Russes superstar Léonide Massine. Captivated by the islands, he made Li Galli his

Between its fame as the legendary haunt of the Sirens – celebrated in Homer's *Odyssey* – and renown as the last home of Rudolf Nureyev, Li Galli's landscape, evergreen with Aleppo pines and Mediterranean maquis, has barely changed.

own island paradise, spending more than fifty years there. Then in 1990, his fellow Russian ballet legend Rudolf Nureyev, apparently dancing to the same tune, chose it as his last home. But in 1996, La Fortuna pointed her finger at a local hotelier named Signor Giovanni Russo, owner of Sorrento's fabled Hotel Bellevue Syrene. He decided to keep everything in the family, so to speak, and paid homage to his hotel's namesake by purchasing the islands from the Nureyev estate.

Today, as in the days of ageless antiquity, the Li Galli islands still have a potent sorcery. Despite the everpresent threat of nature's vagaries, these three islets stand as an iconic presence off Punta Campanella on the Sorrentine peninsula. The trio comprises Gallo Lungo, the largest, which takes the form of a half-moon; the tinier Brigante (also known as Castelluccio for its rock shape); and the nearly circular Rotunda. They look like giant rock anchors, as if without them the mainland would slip its moorings and sail away.

With the implausibility of an oasis in the desert – in this case, a desert of *verde-azzurro* water – they rise out of the sea like some sort of Amalfi atoll. Sitting off the Punta Campanella like a Lilliputian Capri – the real one rises with Gibraltarian bulk on the near horizon – they are small enough to covet yet loom large in the imagination. Though made up of three rocky islets, when seen from the mainland they appear to form a single island, even, from certain vantage points, taking the eerie silhouette of a submerged woman. Little wonder, then, that early seamen nicknamed the group Sirene and regarded it as the haunt of the infamous Sirens, described by Homer in Book XII of the *Odyssey*.

Historians now know that in fact the legend originated in Eastern mythology and was brought eastwards to Greece by the first traders to explore the western Mediterranean, the Phoenicians. Providing a perfect anchorage, Li Galli were frequented by Phoenician merchants en route to Ischia and Positano. Historians' most recent

conclusion is that the name Li Galli does not after all refer to 'roosters', as was once thought – derived from the image (prevalent during the medieval era) of the Sirens as harpy-like creatures with claws – but rather from *gaoul*, the Phoenician word for ship. At some point during the Middle Ages, Li Galli became known as Guallum, echoing the earlier Phoenician name.

During the Greek era, it was from Parthenope, Queen of the Sirens, that nearby Naples obtained her most ancient name. When the ancient Romans took over, the isles were immortalized in the *Aeneid's* tale of the Trojan adventurer whose mythic voyage passed along the Amalfi coast on his way to the mouth of the Tiber. It is said that the Emperor Tiberius and his court often sailed to the *isole* from nearby Capri to see if they could hear the Sirens' song, which some said was really the sound of waves crashing in nearby caves or came from the seals that used to swim in these waters. Then, in the dawn of the Age of Empire, Emperor Frederick II and King Robert

Above left and right: Built to protect these waters from Saracen pirates, the Aragonese Tower – erected in the fifteenth century by the new Spanish rulers of Naples – was transformed by the choreographer and danseur Leonide Massine into a palatial dance studio and residence, and enlarged with a terrace big enough for dance recitals. Above centre: Seen from the Main Terrace on Gallo Lungo, the biggest of the three Li Galli, the islets of Brigante and Rotunda comprise the other two stars of this rocky constellation.

of Anjou established medieval fiefdoms on Li Galli, building up the ancient Roman tower into a fortress to prevent the increasing attacks of marauders.

Because southern Italian trade routes were often plundered by Arab pirates and Turkish privateers, who were drawn by cargoes of silks and spices on vessels sailing from Constantinople to Amalfi – 10 miles/16 kilometres south of Li Galli, Amalfi was the first of the great medieval maritime republics – the Siren myth may simply have been an expression of the terror that gripped sailors who had to cross the pirate-infested sea lanes. This hazard of the sailing life increased after the fall of the Roman Empire, when Roman vessels no longer policed the waters.

Adding to the Siren myth was the troublesome fact that Li Galli lay in becalmed waters between the Bays of Naples and Salerno. Testimony to this is Goethe's letter of 14 May 1787, in which he reports that while returning from Sicily to Naples his boat encountered such a dead calm near Li Galli that the sea currents, always very powerful in this stretch, nearly caused his ship to be wrecked on the Galli shoals. With nary a breeze to fill their sails, sailors felt Li Galli were the Sirens at work, especially when the prevailing wind of summer, the sirocco, 'charmed the waves to sleep'.

The idea of the Sirens – nineteenth-century salon painters pictured them seductively reclining on sea-girt rocks, lyres in hand, clashing cymbals, with jewels and human bones strewn around them – inspired a legion of writers, from Milton to Hans Christian Andersen. The latter was moved to write his *Little Mermaid* tale after a momentous trip to Capri.

In 1996 when 'luckissimo' (his term) Giovanni Russo purchased Li Galli from the estate of Rudolf Nureyev, the great Russian dancer had spent years restoring the islands, devoting special care to the villa and the fifteenth-century Aragonese tower, transforming their interiors with priceless blue-hued nineteenth-century tilework from Seville, a décor that reminded him of the days when architecture along this coastline was influenced by Saracen (Arab) style at the Angevin court in nearby Naples (tiles were needed as the sea air here is ruinous to paint). But Signor Russo is the first to acknowledge that, like three diamonds in the rough, Li Galli were guided to a large extent from mine to finished jewels by the danseur Léonide Massine.

Today Massine is known most widely for his role as the Shoemaker in *The Red Shoes* – the 1948 award-winning film for which he also choreographed the eponymous ballet danced by its star, Moira Shearer – but the roots of his legendary status are the many roles he brilliantly portrayed while he was the leading danseur for Diaghilev's Ballets Russes, starring in several ballets based on Neapolitan themes, such as *La Boutique Fantasque*, *Insalata* and *Pulcinella*. His infatuation with Li Galli began in 1919, while the troupe was performing in Naples and he was staying with a friend in Positano (his travelling companions were fellow artists Picasso and Cocteau), from where he first spied the islands. For him they 'had all the drama and mystery of a painting by Salvatore Rosa', and he acquired them in 1922.

Massine's early efforts at improvement proved to be a disappointing and unrequited labour of love. Friends derided the land as horticulturally challenged, fit only for 'fig trees and rabbits', but after learning that the islands' soil was equal in fertility to Capri's, Massine determined to cajole it into tractability. He first had to win a tug of war with the *tramontana* that blew off the Lattari peaks on the mainland. While this bitter north wind destroyed hundreds of the pine trees he planted, cypresses thrived, as did fig and juniper trees. This made him realize that he should use only species native to the region, since they could withstand the elements. These mainly comprised indigenous plants of the *macchia mediterranea* or maquis: sun-loving species like rosemary, santolina and lavender, which do not have to be watered.

Massine's main focus was the plateau, the only flat patch on the see-sawing terrain of the island; this was more or less level with the front of the ruined Roman villa, and had once been a Roman *xystus* or garden. Sure of success, he planted rows of trimmed myrtle and rosemary bushes. He restored four 1,300-foot/400-metre-long garden terraces (which helped buttress the terrain) at the northern stern of the island, beneath the Aragonese tower, and covered them with grape vines from Sicily and vegetable varieties imported from nurseries in Rome and Florence.

Turning to the housing situation, Massine first restored the fortress-like tower, installing a fully equipped dance studio, complete with Siberian pinewood floor, on the second floor. Next, he ambitiously proceeded to build a villa, with the design advice of the

Once the site of an ancient Roman villa and garden, the Main Terrace now has a fountain blooming with water lilies and decorated by Rudolf Nureyev with Arab–Hispano tilework.

great Le Corbusier, on the ruined site of the ancient Roman *domus*. Inside, the finished décor was an eclectic assemblage of Moorish tiles and Chippendale chairs, to provide suitable surroundings for such illustrious guests as the composers Stravinsky and Hindemith. Despite the resulting grandeur of the villa, however, the real show was outside. At twilight, Massine would shepherd his guests to a large portico overlooking the main garden, where all would silently watch the sun grow lower in the sky over Capri. Not a word was spoken throughout the hour until the sun had set; then they would all go in to a festive dinner.

Stupendo is the term to describe the Cinerama-like vista, which ranges from Capri to Cape Licosa at the end of the Sorrentine peninsula. It is a landscape in which time as we know it is suspended; Odysseus could sail these waters again and feel right at home. As was the case for thousands of years, not a single house can be seen. In fact, the only building that ever stood on the peninsula's headland was a now-vanished temple to Athene, built by the ancient Greeks,

'You can be at home with Homer here!' states current owner Signor Giovanni Russo, who fully intends to protect this landscape from development. Happily, the surrounding vista will remain forever green, as much of the Punta Campanella region is now a nature reserve.

who always built such temples in places of spectacular natural beauty. Happily, this vista will stay forever green and undeveloped, for it was recently made into a protected marine area, the Area Marina Protetta Punta Campanella.

'In such a consecrated landscape, it is important not to "gardenize" nature too much,' says Signor Russo. 'Thanks to the desalinization plant that Rudolf Nureyev installed on the island, we could have imported any exotic species under the sun – water is no longer a problem. But I feel this garden should remain *primordiale*. Granted, it takes a lot of work to look "natural". And we do have carefully cultivated *giardinetti* of succulents and herbs. But these islands need to stay connected with nature, to be at one with this mythical landscape. You can be at home with Homer here!'

Like Massine and Nureyev, Signor Russo finds Li Galli a place of sublime tranquillity. Massine may have initially come here in order to escape, but he wound up finding the *isole* a great source of inspiration. Here he could choreograph his ballets and write his books, including *My Life in Ballet* (1968), in which he writes, 'Li Galli brought me closer to a life of simplicity, offering a kind of spiritual peace and serenity which I have never found anywhere else. It was always more than just a place of refuge; it represented something in my life which I had yet to discover.'

With indulgently solicitous care, Signor Russo has owned and run a number of famous hotels – his newest, Hotel Ville Tre Ville, being the former home of Franco Zeffirelli (imagine the décor!), just outside Positano – spending years in the midst of celebrity, glamour and high style. Never more so than in his stewardship of the Bellevue Syrene, Sorrento's most legendarily soigné hotel, where he lives a life *en majesté* – almost literally. With murals painted to make the 1860s King of Bavaria feel at home, and an ambience so *chez soi* that Empress Eugénie of France overstayed her week by three months, this Sorrento landmark is a fantasia of Venetian chandeliers, Louis-Phillipe rugs and Belle Epoque salons. (The consummate hotelier, Russo has charmingly tweaked the classically lush interiors with a new sprinkle of modern glasswork, art photography and hip armoires.) The beautiful people head here to holiday, but for his own holiday, Signor Russo heads to Li Galli, which he too values for '*una semplicità della vita*'.

So respectful is he of the elements that make up this natural treasure that he wears his island role as a curator-protector-conservator humbly. Whether playing host to a family group or to close friends like actor Harrison Ford or Microsoft founder Paul Allen, he takes his cue from the tiny bluebacks that are native to the islands: 'We are all lizards. The tempo of life must be ancient – calm and slow – and we each must have our own space to disappear to.' Signor Russo disappears into the vegetable gardens beneath the Aragonese tower, where he harvests courgettes, aubergines and his favourite Cuore di Bue cherry tomatoes. Near by are his animals, including Rosina, his beloved donkey. For spiritual serenity, he repairs to a small, beautiful chapel – a miniature version of a Greek church – which he has built at the southern end of the island. But to really feel 'happissimo' he just dives into the sea. Alternately soothed and energized by its warm and cold currents, he soon feels the spell of the islands working. The Sirens' song lulls him into castaway mode. But then, invariably, a little voice whispers John Donne's caveat that 'No man is an island' and he's off and running back to Sorrento.

La Bella Sorrento

Villa Silvana

Sorrento

'The most beautiful place on earth' was the phrase used by the nineteenth-century French novelist Stendhal to describe Sorrento and even the most travel-hardened today may agree with him. Italy at its time-faded, pastel-hued Belle Epoque best, Sorrento is charmingly decked out with churches with Rococo trim, continental cafés shaded by tomato-orange awnings and alley views that echo the sepia-tinted photographs of old – except for the ever-present mounds of pink bougainvillea. Surrounded as it is by orange and lemon groves and sheltered by the Lattari mountains, and with a view of the Bay of Naples that has been straining the vocabulary of travellers ever since Odysseus was nearly ensnared by the call of the Sirens, it is little wonder that scores of visitors return year after year to the chorus line of grand hotels perched along the bay.

For a lucky few, however, the town is home year round. While the most celebrated curve of the bay is the address of such landmark hotels as the Excelsior Vittoria and Bellevue Syrene, there remain, scattered here and there, a handful of private villas. The Villa Silvana is one of these, enjoying an idyllic perch directly above the Marina Piccola.

Gates open to reveal an exceedingly pretty white villa, impressive enough to have housed the American consulate around the turn of the twentieth century. The driveway is framed by *Washingtonia* palms and a dense planting of oleander and holm oaks, but this is merely an introduction to the main show: it is only when one rounds the rear of the villa that the picture-perfect vista of the Bay of Naples comes into view. Reminding us of the phrase Stadius used when writing about the villa of Pollius Felix (the ruins of which on the nearby Campanella promontory are still a top attraction), '*in vertice Surrentino*', not only does the estate sit enthroned at the top of Sorrento's tableland but its garden also hugs the precipitous hillside 300 feet/90 metres down to the water, the last estate in Sorrento still to do this.

When Signora Silvana Pane d'Esposito acquired the estate in 1970, she found to her delight an expanded and renovated domicile,

with the compliments of the American consulate. In contrast, the orchards – its *raison d'être* when the property functioned as a *masserie* (farm) – had been left irreversibly neglected, the practice of diplomacy not being dependent on a ready supply of oranges and lemons. Wisely choosing to put her efforts into replacement rather than restoration, the signora drew up an ambitious plan for a flower garden, to be framed and interspersed with impressively towering trees. Patience is deemed a virtue, but try telling that to a passionate visionary such as the signora. Realizing that she could not hurry Mother Nature but determined to see results *pronto*, she had mature tree specimens brought in, along with the tractors necessary to plant them. With these in place, the signora was content to allow other specimens, including baby olive trees (gleaned from her mother's garden), to grow as seedlings.

Sitting at the tables on the terrace, guests gape at the bay view, which is strikingly accented by a white classical balustrade topped by terracotta urns abloom with camellias, the only note of colour in the garden. 'It's true, I'm basically a greenie,' Signora Silvana exclaims. 'Though I love them all, I don't have a favourite flower, but green is my colour.' Supporting her claim are the countless plants packed into the gardens that are squeezed along the cliff face, the almost jungle-like density of plants providing shade from the Sorrento sun in any season.

While it is set alluringly by the bay, the lush Villa Silvana garden is reminiscent of one of Sorrento's most remarkable natural features: its fern-draped romantic glens, filled with greenery. The

Sitting high atop the Sorrentine escarpment, the main terrace of Villa Silvana offers a verdant frame of dwarf palms, camellias and geraniums to the view over the Bay of Naples.

Left: Essentially a five-storey belvedere to the gulf view, the villa garden is connected by a zigzagging stairway that ambles through an arcaded gallery past rock faces green with Japanese creeper (*Parthenocissus tricuspidata*). Above: The Main Terrace flaunts a view that invites guests, according to Signora Pane d'Esposito, 'to perfect the three L's: Look, Laze, and Linger!' Right: The stairway down to the water is embowered with dense foliage which dramatizes the surprise views of the bay below.

most beautiful of these – often containing a jungle of foliage – are the rocky ravines that pierce the Sorrento tableland. Local lore says these are the haunts of pixies, called Monacelli by the Sorrentines. Signora Silvana has never spotted any of these elfin spirits but says they have a standing invitation to visit her garden.

Zigzagging their way along five terraced levels, the narrow and steeply inclined garden steps echo the *vicoletti*, the steep rocky paths on many of Sorrento's surrounding hills. Climbing them requires balance, as some acrobatics are needed to bend beneath overgrown branches or step gingerly around extended palm fronds. As you begin the cliffside descent, you pass through a gorgeous stone gallery, its columns providing frames for the bay vista. Soon, a balcony set with table and chairs comes into view. Or nearly: it is almost smothered by shade-loving plants and diminutive ferns, providing a green and embowered retreat that is typically southern Italian in its happy carelessness. Peeking through the foliage, of course, is the mesmerizing bay vista, once again: the garden is basically a five-level belvedere from which to enjoy the view. Guests and family – Signora Silvana's two sisters, Rosa and Rita, own two of Sorrento's most

historic estates, the Villa Rosa and the Villa Astor – never fail to enjoy the deliciously seductive beauty of the Villa Silvana. Overlooking what the nineteenth-century explorer Heinrich Schliemann once called 'the finest view in the world', it is a haven designed to satisfy perfectly one's inclination for looking, lazing and lingering.

A Regal Realm

Parco dei Principi

Sant'Agnello

*B*asking in the genial warmth of the sun, its air redolent with orange blossom and cooled by breezes from the Bay of Naples, Sorrento has long been considered a horticultural *piccolo paradiso*. The legend of the Sorrentine peninsula as a paradise took root in the sixteenth century, when its natural lushness inspired native son Torquato Tasso to set his tales of the star-crossed lovers Rinaldo and Armida in magnificent garden-like settings. When Grand Tour sightseers – such as Lord Byron, the Duke of Wellington, Sir Walter Scott and Goethe – caught up with the region's allure in the nineteenth century, Sorrento became a stage for the idyll rich. Before long, the entire peninsula was settled with many magnificent garden estates. Unfortunately, Sorrento was also engulfed by palatial hotels, built to accommodate the rush of wealthy khans, shahs and princes. As a result, thousands of travellers throng Sorrento today, many of whom have come in search of the now mostly vanished palmy and balmy never-never land of yore.

But for a memorable replay of Sorrento's Edenic past, there is the charming hamlet of Sant'Agnello, a mere thirty-minute walk – yet a world away – from the town's central Piazza Tasso. Here the historic Parco dei Principi awaits to satisfy all one's visions of a sweet, sun-kissed Sorrento. Hidden in mysterious luxuriance behind a wrought-iron gate, the garden remains the best-preserved sanctuary of all. It took a pair of rich-as-Croesus individuals – one from the royal Bourbon line, followed by one from the Russian nobility – to nurture this park into the cornucopia of rare species it is today. High on the clifftop and facing the Bay of Naples, as well as a brooding Vesuvius, this paean to Romanticism still embodies the nineteenth-century ideal of natural beauty.

Right and opposite: Built up around the bayside villa of Poggio Siracusa, the estate was designed in 1792 as a courtly retreat for Count Paolo-Leopoldo di Siracusa, a Bourbon cousin of the king of Naples.

Embowered by hundreds of exotic trees, and threaded by shady, twisting walks that pass leafy nooks at every twist, this is a garden made for dalliance, and it is therefore fitting that it was laid out around an offering – sacrificial, as it turns out – of a neo-classical-style Temple of Love, built by the park's first private owner, Count Paolo-Leopoldo di Siracusa, a Bourbon cousin of Ferdinand IV, the King of Naples.

The count acquired the estate when the park's former owners, the Jesuits, were driven from Italy by royal fiat. He proceeded to transform the old vegetable garden of the Cocumella monastery into a pleasure garden and made further improvements to the estate, especially the erection at the cliff's edge of a grand villa ornamented with frolicking cupids, airy balustrades, royal crests and floors of Capodimonte porcelain.

He constructed his elegant *tempietto* on the spot where once grew the 'bloom of eternal love' – and thereby hangs a tale. Back in the early eighteenth century, a monk from the monastery, one Friar Zaccaria, had returned from a mission in the Peruvian Andes and brought back with him the 'plant of Eros', as he called it, which he replanted in the grounds far from the eyes of the Father Superior. Extolling the properties of what we now know to be cocaine, the monk was soon silenced as a heretic and promptly expired (in, it was noted, an 'ecstatic death').

Eager to banish such dark tales, the count also bedecked the park surrounding the *tempietto*, importing many rare species, including a majestic allée of *Washingtonia* palms, all to make a suitable setting for the young noblewoman who was the love of his life. One Easter day, however, he learned that his beloved Tania had died back home on a visit to Russia and he went mad with grief. Their butterfly world had come to an end but their tragic love is still commemorated in the marble Temple of Love, which today nests in a froth of pink and violet hydrangea (best in mid-summer and early autumn).

As with all the flowers in this park, these blossoms are ensured shade because the trees provide a canopy of leaves that allows in

Above left: Close by the count's Rococo-style villa is this elegiac fountain which poignantly memorializes his tragic love affair with a Russian noblewoman. Above centre: This fountain is embowered with elephant ears (*Colocasia esculenta*). Right: Fine specimens of magnolia shade guests as Canary palms (*Phoenix canariensis*) catch their eyes. Overleaf: With a passion that foresaw only happy endings, Count Paolo-Leopoldo commissioned this Temple of Love, which today is surrounded by spectacular hydrangeas and hortensias.

just the right amount of sunshine. Exotic specimens such as *Jubaea spectabilis*, *Araucaria bidwillii* and *Chamaerops humilis* tower over the park's two main roads, the Viale dei Cavalieri and the Viale delle Felci (*felci* meaning ferns), which invitingly run through the garden and continue down to the belvedere terrace overlooking the bay. From these main roads smaller paths meander this way and that, drawing visitors who might be inclined to dally in leafy nooks sheltered by growths of *Syagrus romanzoffiana*, *Pachypodium lamerei* and *Cocculus laurifolius*. One such path leads to the evocatively named Ponticello dell'Amore, which spans a stream that flows from a swan pond to a nineteenth-century grotto. The bridge is inscribed with the words of a poem by Napoleon's first amour, Desirée, a frequent visitor to this dell. Venturing on to the close-shaven lawns near by brings you face to face with some of the rare plantings Desireé may have seen during her walks: *Phoenix reclinata*, *Ginkgo biloba* and *Agathis dammara*.

With the arrival of Garibaldi on the scene, the Bourbons fled and the count's Villa of Poggio Siracusa fell into disrepair. Decades later it was sold to the first of several Russian noble families, who, *choix de soleil*, wished to exchange their chilly homeland for the soft Sorrentine sun. Just in time to revive the ailing property, a second Croesus stepped into the picture, in 1885. This was Prince Constantino Cortchacow, a Russian noble with connections to the reigning tsar. He, in turn, bequeathed the villa to a daughter, Princess Elena.

This lady was a botanical snob who shunned local species, preferring instead to spend unreasonable sums on exotica such as *Podocarpus totara*, *Liriodendron tulipifera*, *Cocculus laurifolius* and *Platanus orientalis*. Her contrariness caused some major casualties, particularly many birch trees imported from Russia, which could not thrive because of the considerable climatic differences between the locales. Meanwhile, competition had broken out between the princess and Lord William Waldorf Astor – then creating his own Villa Tritone extravaganza on the other side of town – with each striving to bag the rarest specimens.

Despite the power of her adversary, the princess managed to hold her own and before long, the transformation of the grounds of the Villa Cortchacow were judged complete and worthy of inspection. On view were a forest of exotic trees, hillocks abloom with blue agapanthus and flower beds bursting with spendthrift quantities of African poppies. On 1 April 1893, the princess rested her watering can to celebrate the reopening of the villa. The fête was attended by Alexandra of Hesse, the future tsarina of Russia; Princess Maud,

soon to become Queen of Sweden; the Duke of York, later to be George V of England; and other crowned luminaries. The party toured the park, with a glass of rose vodka in one hand, a saucer of caviar cannelloni in the other, and agreed that the results of the transformation were magnificent.

The current owners of the Hotel Parco dei Principi, the Royal Continental Group, are determined to preserve the garden's history, looking on it as a *jardin-musée*. The garden staff – a father-and-son team with nearly fifty years' combined service – do a thorough annual pruning after the June flowering and keep up with occasional excess palm growth (they have saved many of the palms from the beetle *Rhynchophorus ferrugineus*, a blight which at the time of writing is afflicting these trees in parts of Campania). Primarily, they think of themselves as plant-preservationists, but when the need arises they will effect major changes, such as replacing the hotel's historic winter garden (its vast collection of roses succumbed to the salty bay air) with a giant pool.

They rejoice in keeping the park's *temps perdu* ambience. Perfect for dallying, the park is a ravishingly beautiful setting in spectacular contrast to the shimmering white-and-blue hotel, designed by Gio Ponti in 1961. Lucky guests here can enjoy the best of both worlds: a sleek Modernist monument and a neo-Renaissance villa, surrounded by a time-burnished garden whose perpetual peace and beauty can be scarcely surpassed in paradise.

A grand allée of Washingtonia palms leads to the swimming pool, once the swannery built for the Bourbon count.

IV

LA DIVINA COSTIERA

The Amalfi Coast

La Dolce Vista

Il San Pietro
Positano

Cool water tickles your toes, sparkling white wine caresses your throat, bougainvillea blossoms flutter at your ear as you bend over the azure pool. Gone are the frown, the bored pout, the red alert of yesterday. 'Hello, gorgeous,' you purr. Fairy godmothers come in many forms and this one is the Hotel Il San Pietro in Positano, considered by many to be the most gigglingly gorgeous hotel on the Amalfi coast. Perched 340 feet/100 metres atop a rocky spur above the Bay of Positano, it enjoys what must be the perfect view of the beloved resort. From a front-row seat on the hotel's grand terrace you can see practically the entire town: sherbet-hued houses tucked cheek-to-cheek into a steep slope that ends at the sea, with a backdrop of palms swaying in a perpetual-motion skyline, and a dense patchwork of bougainvillea, dichondra and fuchsia, all vying for space on the hillside.

A real cliff-hanger of an address, the San Pietro is built on the spot – marked by an eighteenth-century chapel – where St Peter's fishing boat first touched land in Italy. But if the saint set foot on this rocky shore today, he would not recognize it: gone is the rugged, Cyclopean rock face that once greeted him and in its place is a profusion of terraced gardens that probably outdo those of Babylon. These are the luxuriant gardens of San Pietro which, covering nearly the entire hill with a sprawling array of blooms in myriad shades of shell pink, ultra-violet, saffron yellow and orchid blue, transform the hotel into a gigantic bouquet.

Acclaimed as the architectural wonder of the coast, the hotel was first envisioned by Carlo Cinque in the early 1960s. He wanted to build a private villa to use as a retreat from his work at the Hotel Miramare, located in the centre of town (which, as one of Positano's hotel-industry pioneers, he had opened in 1934). Space and light were in

Nearly levitating over the Bay of Positano and planted with an orchidaceous array of flowers, the Grand Terrace is one of the most glamorous spots on earth.

short supply in the mountain-hugging town, but he eventually found both on some land on the peak of a cliff-face 2 miles/3 kilometres south, in the Laurito district, where the mountains are steepest. Before long, he had built a small apartment and garden there; he then added other rooms and terraces, imaginatively blending them in with the landscape. The results being unexpectedly promising, the idea of transforming his private domain into a hotel began to take shape. Carlo plunged forward with the project, spending eight years in the 1960s dynamiting the mountain apart and then the next three years putting everything back together. Signora Virginia Attanasio Cinque, his niece and now owner of the hotel, remembers: 'Carlino would often take his boat out into the bay to determine how he needed to carve, plant and sculpt the San Pietro hill.'

When the Hotel Il San Pietro officially opened, in late 1970, it was revealed as being like a mini-Positano, with thirty-three guest rooms astonishingly staggered over a dozen cantilevered ledges, with balconies covered in cascades of bougainvillea. The hotel quickly became a *ne plus ultra* for patrons seeking unlimited beauty and pampering, all lavishly on hand thanks to the magnificent accommodation: suites uniquely decorated with headboards made from gilded Baroque altars, painted eighteenth-century armoires and hand-made Vietri tiles, and a seaside restaurant (accessed by a lift blasted into the rock), where pampered patrons could dine on champagne and rosemary risotto. Voluptuaries favoured the suites furnished with faun-shaped bath taps that dispensed *acqua* in wicked ways, while topping even that entertaining touch was the so-called 'room without a number', equipped with a full-sized statue of a eunuch whose artistically wrought organ had the gift of dispensing water (a Union Jack to drape over the protrusion was available by request). Before long many illustrious guests, including Princess Caroline of Monaco, the Rockefellers, Rudolf Nureyev, Gregory Peck, Barbra Streisand, the King of Jordan, Giovanni Agnelli and Julia Roberts, were enjoying the delights and wonders of the hotel.

But the most beloved 'guests' for Carlo Cinque were his flowers. In such a confined space, with the Amalfi Drive at one end and the cliff edge at the other, he had to focus his energies on floral blooms, not lawns, hills and dells. As a result, the garden, fronting the grand terrace just outside the main lobby, is one of the most orchidaceous patches found on this earth. Begonias, roses, jasmines and hibiscus representing every tint of the rainbow create a brilliant canopy of colour that jostles against another layer of blossoms: massed beds of nasturtiums, bluebells and morning glories. In one corner, pink, wine-red and white oleanders nod next to trumpets of *Datura*

Left: Leading from the Grand Terrace to the main lobby is a path lined with multicoloured touch-me-nots (*Impatiens*). Dichondra is planted between the paving stones. Above: A principal focal point on the upper patios is the Chinese hibiscus.

suaveolens. Exploding near by along a stone pathway are blood-red fuchsias and pink and white petunias, while magenta, orange and red poppies frame a great view of Positano. Centre stage here is the spectacular floss-silk tree (*Chorisia speciosa*), laden from June to August with candy-pink flowers similar to those of oriental lilies. Every great show has a spectacular production number and the San Pietro's is the dancing cascades of sun-lit bougainvillea, from whose advance no balcony or path appears to be safe. 'Even when the day is rainy, it is always a Technicolor extravaganza here,' says Signora Cinque with a smile.

'Carlo practised ecology before there was such a thing,' she continues. 'He taught me that it is most important to kiss the flowers, not just rip them out of the earth.' To create his little Eden, he first made a list of plant vegetation growing in Positano, as he insisted on

giving any endangered species a safe haven. And to make a garden where there had once been only rock, he bought soil from other construction projects in Positano, in support of his belief that "soil is more valuable than gold".'

Since there wasn't a sufficient quantity of soil to begin with, Cinque decided to that he had to find a way to encourage the outdoors to come in. So he drilled through walls, ceilings and floors, and famously threaded vines and creepers through the openings, training them to grow in from the outside. In one room, an entire ceiling is embroidered with a spreading *Ficus benjamina*. In many salons, *Philodendron pertusum* creeps up the walls. The pillars in the main lobby are laced over with an abundance of bougainvillea, whose lush twinings combine with a vast expanse of glass windows to give the lobby the appearance of a greenhouse. In fact, when the hotel closes for the winter (from December to February), it more or less functions as one: all the potted plants, high-maintenance blooms and special-care ferns are moved there for the duration. Colonized by these tender plants, the lobby – its part-DeMille, part-de Milo décor ripe with antique nude statues and gilded antiques – makes one ponder if the San Pietro is technically more vegetable than

Opposite: the Upper Patio is home to hundreds of *Salvia splendens* and red and yellow *Lantana camara* surrounding the *Cycas revoluta* in the centre. Positano can be seen in the background. Above: The famed majolica settees created by Fratelli Stingo – inspired by the majolica benches in the Chiostro delle Clarisse in Naples's Santa Chiara – are divided by terracotta urns filled with flowers that annually change from summer to summer: here, in 2009, on show are firecracker plants (*Russelia equisetiformis*) from Mexico.

mineral. With a sparkle in her eye, Signora Cinque remembers that 'during winter months, Carlo imagined the plants reproaching him for their isolation, so he would go around complimenting them until guests could arrive again'.

The hotel is surrounded by verdant hillside, a section of which Signora Cinque has put to use as her private vegetable 'patch'. Established decades before sustainability became a byword in gardening, this is basically a cliff-side tower of five enormous terraces planted with tomatoes, aubergines and herbs (lots of Mediterranean

Below: Succulents from North America are found in planters on the Grand Terrace's tables. Right: A lemon tree frames a view of the Bay of Positano.

myrtle, basil and rosemary), and the lucky guests of the San Pietro's Michelin-starred restaurant enjoy its harvest.

But the glory of the San Pietro remains its incomparable show of shows, the long-running floral pageant which alone brings guests back for many a return visit. They often come to sit on the magnificent majolica benches of the hotel's grand terrace, which offers a cliff-side perch over the water. Carlino was inspired to create these famous banquettes when, tired of constantly replacing the cushions on the terrace chairs after a rainstorm, he sought a more permanent solution. Remembering the enchanting majolica cloister of Naples's Santa Chiara church, in 1984 he commissioned Fratelli Stingo to create the eleven benches, whose faience-painted pictures depict maritime scenes in seventeenth-century fashion. Here, you will often find guests raising a glass of the hotel's signature drink – a refreshing blend of lemon juice, mineral water and almond syrup mysteriously dubbed 'elephant's milk' – in homage to the hotel's creator, Carlino Cinque.

Above left: Many guest-room balconies at the San Pietro are bordered by magnificent displays of bougainvillea and hibiscus. Above right: Even the entryway is a floral extravaganza. Opposite: All guests can enjoy the grand panorama of Positano that a lucky few, right, can savour from grand suites whose balconies are often arboured with masses of begonias, jasmines, nasturtiums and oleanders.

Blossom Fever

Palazzo Murat

Positano

'The Italian garden does not exist for its flowers,' wrote Edith Wharton in *Italian Villas and Their Gardens* (1904). 'Its flowers exist for it; they are a late and infrequent adjunct to its beauties, a parenthetical grace counting only as one more touch in the general effect of enchantment.'

Mrs Wharton would probably have reconsidered her use of the word 'parenthetical' if she ever had called at the courtyard garden of the Palazzo Murat in Positano. Step through the entrance portal of this eighteenth-century Versailles clone – an imposing structure in Neapolitan Baroque attributed to Luigi Vanvitelli (famed for designing the vast palace at Caserta, north of Naples) – and you enter a patio that seems to be home to three-quarters of the most colourful flowers in the world. With a palette that would shame even the French Impressionists, shimmering in sunlight, this garden is a riotous conflagration of blooms.

Honeysuckle and and passionflower tumble down the ancient palazzo walls. Jasmine and strelitzia form a coverlet over stone staircases. Profuse growths of jasmine creep up trellises. Trails of nasturtiums sway from balcony to balcony. And everywhere there is neon-pink bougainvillea. Growing in astounding luxuriance – it embowers doorways, interlaces various terraces and completely canopies the 'downtown Positano' street outside – it has made Palazzo Murat into a shrine for bougainvillea idoltry. As if all this were not enough, amidst it stands one of the world's most beautiful trees: *Chorisia speciosa*. A tree whose wow factor is such that it could stand alone, it is called in local terminology *paloboraccio* ('falling down drunk'), because, like the hibiscus, its huge candy-pink blossoms drop immediately after blooming.

Clearly, the lavish abundance of flowers here reveals the extent to which nature can combine hues without jarring on the eye. If you are blossom hungry – and we are talking thousands here – a visit will give a mood lift like no other. 'Let the day be grey – no matter,' says Mrs Marilu Attanasio, who, with her husband Mario, has transformed the Palazzo Murat into one of Italy's most admired luxury hotels. As her eye falls on the Technicolored cataracts of bougainvillea, she notes, 'Believe me, we don't have to worry about midwinter gaiety here! It almost feels like summer all year long.'

While the garden's origins go back centuries, like most growing things it is still 'unfinished'. Nearly every week finds changes afoot: species being transplanted from one plot to another, a new fruit patch being squeezed in, 'Fireworks' solidago being planted for the first time. She is always experimenting for, as she puts it, 'You must fall in love before you get married.'

Mrs Attanasio grew up in the Palazzo Murat. Her grandfather, Giacomo (along with most of Positano), emigrated to America at the beginning of the twentieth century. Making good, he returned in triumph to his hometown, married Concette and then bought the palazzo in 1905 for their growing and extended family. 'Grandfather grew everything but flowers,' Mrs Attanasio reminisces. 'His "garden" was half vegetable patch, half vineyard; we used to press the grapes in the *saloni* on the palazzo's first floor. Flowers – then considered precious because they required so much water, a luxury in this part of the world – had no place. In that era, of course, you did not buy tomatoes, potatoes or courgettes: you grew them.' In the 1950s, his heirs took over and opened the palazzo as a hotel.

Sitting at the very centre of Positano – 'the only town in the world conceived on a vertical rather than a horizontal axis', to quote the painter Paul Klee – the Palazzo Murat exults in the ultimate luxury hereabouts: ample space. In a town where tumbledown houses are piled on top of each other as they leapfrog their way up the steep inclines of Monti Commune and Sant'Angelo, the palazzo sits on

One of Italy's leading shrines for bougainvillea idolatry, the Palazzo Murat has cascades of *Bougainvillea spectabilis* covering its walls, balconies and terraces.

the 'Piazza San Marco' of Positano: a nearly flat 8-acre/3-hectare parcel of land within the shadow of the cupola of Santa Maria Assunta, which hovers over Positano's Spaggia Grande beach.

When the church was being rebuilt in the eighteenth century, the Frati Benedettini decided they needed a monastery, and that is how the palazzo began life. Vanvitelli (or his atelier) whipped up a slice of architectural paradise for the Benedictine brothers, although the only motifs that still remind us of this era are the pilgrims' 'shells of St James' carved on the balcony fronts. The monastery must have been startling, rising as it did out of what was then a seaside village of fishermen's shacks. When Joachim Murat, Napoleon's brother-in-law, became King of Naples in 1808, he began to close down various religious orders and, in need of a place where he and his wife, Principessa Caroline Bonaparte, could escape the rigours of rule (and overheated Naples), he decided to make it his *pied à mer*, importing Empire-style brocades for the walls and fancy opulent

Opposite: The eighteenth-century monastery building is often trimmed with festive bougainvillea, as the flowering season stretches from May to December. The Palazzo Murat's 'Sanderiana' variety blooms all year round and so requires a regular 'coiffure', often supplied by a talented sculptor from nearby Praiano. Above: This view seen from Upper Positano shows how the garden park of the Palazzo Murat forms a green hub to the lower town. Overleaf left: The Upper Patio of the Palazzo Murat garden leads down to a lower level, formerly the orchard of the monastery and now planted with an array of herbs, vegetables, fruit and flowers which are all used in the dishes served by the hotel's noted restaurant. Overleaf right: Surrounding one of the hotel's unique Vietri-sculpted terracotta busts which line the lower garden is a bouquet of gorgeously coloured blossoms.

furnishings for the rooms, giving it all the comforts of back home. Unfortunately, 'Gioacchino' Murat proved more of a fop than a war hero (he was notorious for riding into battle bare-chested when not decked out in one of his gilded uniforms); within fifteen years, his French forces had been routed from Naples, ending his dreams of a Neapolitan kingdom. He stepped before a British firing squad in 1817.

Today Wall Streeters, deadline slaves and other weary workers escape to the Hotel Palazzo Murat for the same reason as the erstwhile King of Naples: to live like fishermen because fishermen – thanks to the awestriking natural beauty of the place – in Positano lived like kings.

Mrs Attanasio says of her garden, 'You would think this is a high-maintenance garden. But it is really no care, no fuss; it just has fantastic flowers, one after the other. The only trouble is that July and August can be diabolically sunny. For a while we were almost tempted to give more water to our flowers than to our guests! But we surmounted this problem by renovating the property's underground cisterns. They were first excavated back in the ancient Roman era, when this entire patch of land was part of an immense *villa marittima*, which was reputedly destroyed by the eruption of Vesuvius in 79 AD. For centuries, the cisterns were used to store wine. We changed that to water, giving us a plentiful supply even on *giornati torridi* (the hottest days).'

The abundant what-others-take-five-years-to-grow-I-can-do-in-one richness of the soil here was one reason why Mrs Attanasio decided to devote half her garden to fruit and vegetables 'that pay the rent': heirloom potatoes, 'Rampicante' courgettes, Roma tomatoes and 'Fire Candle' radishes, as well as the bounty from fruit trees, such as figs, guavas, lemons, oranges and even a feijoa, often wind up among the gustatory delights of the hotel's highly rated Al Palazzo restaurant. The vegetable garden is right by the restaurant, and if you order the chef's famous dessert of green basil ice cream with red alpine fingernail-sized *fragoline di bosco* (wild strawberries), all suspended in an effervescent jelly made from sparkling red wine, you'll probably spot the patches where the basil and strawberries grew. This is 'sustainability', albeit on a very elegant scale. 'Hard work? It probably takes me less time to garden than to shop in a supermarket,' Mrs Attanasio says with a laugh.

In the palazzo's courtyard, one of the most magnificent bougainvilleas in Italy seems to climb the walls of the eighteenth-century building.

The only high-maintenance item is the famous bougainvillea. 'The Sanderiana species we have here blooms all year round, and at some point we have to give them a "coiffure".' To trim them back just so, Mrs Attanasio engages a sculptor based in nearby Praiano. 'He has just the right *potatura* (touch). We usually do this in July, when the plants tend to get *secca* (dry). He just picks all the vines clean of dessicated leaves, and they all merrily continue to flower, right up to Christmas, when we like to make trees and wreaths from the blossoms.'

A slow walk up the garden path reveals two levels. The upper terrace is the floral patio. Stone steps descend to the lower patio, home to the restaurant; this leads to the vegetable garden, which is shaded by fruit trees and bordered by a collection of aloe and agave succulents and cacti. The eye is excited wherever it falls. Sweet rows of elegant gourmet lettuces give way to trombone squash, all so picturesquely lovely that one forgets whether vegetables are utilitarian or artistic – whether they should be eaten or just looked at.

Having recently returned from a holiday in Thailand, Mrs Attanasio has just planted a species of ginger, which blooms with an immense red flower. 'And this is not as exotic as you might think: remember that frangipani, a staple of Italian gardens, was originally imported from Siam.' Mrs Attanasio always travels with her cutting knife. 'I'm always looking for something new,' she says. 'It is only by means of constant shifting and rearrangement that we come closer to our ideal. On the other hand, I like change so much, I'm not really into perfection.' Forever tweaking her plant combinations, she knows her garden will always be in a state of evolution. In this she follows in her mother's footsteps. 'Mamma loved this garden – she was out here by seven in the morning and didn't stop until five at night.' As for Mrs Attanasio: 'My hands give you the answer.' With such devotion and love lavished on it, it is no wonder that the Palazzo Murat garden is of such an exuberantly rich lushness and floral beauty.

Opposite: Petunias and roses are just a few of the vibrant flowers that make the Palazzo Murat garden a feast for the eyes. Left: Amphorae are scattered throughout the lower garden, serving to remind guests that the history of the palazzo extends back to the days of the ancient Roman Empire.

The Flower and the Glory
Villa Rufolo
Ravello

Step on to the upper terrace of the Villa Rufolo and before you is a vista that defines the colour blue once and for all. A veil of celestial hue extends as far as the eye can see. Its pearly transparency clarifies and defines a panorama of the Bay of Salerno to a fare-thee-well, from the reach-out-and-touch cupolas of Santissima Annunziata to the distant shores of ancient Paestum. The vista almost upstages one of the most magnificent gardens in Italy: several garden terraces which, hanging upon a spur of Monte Cerreto as if meditating a plunge into the sea 1,400 feet/425 metres below, amphitheatrically encompass this breathtaking panorama where sky and sea seem to merge. With all paradise seemingly spread out before you – the infinitude of hues has often been called 'the bluest view in the world' – drifts of cloud seem to be your only link to the great cosmos. Even in a region where such moments are commonplace, this vision of beauty takes everyone's breath away.

It is little mystery, then, why Lorenzo Rufolo – whom Boccaccio used as the basis for a tale about one of Italy's richest men in his *Decameron* – chose this eagle's nest for his thirteenth-century Scheherazadian extravaganza. With its Arab–Norman tower, Moorish cloisters and gardens fit for a pope (His Eminence Pope Hadrian IV, to be precise, who, legend has it, planted some of the old rose gardens), the Villa Rufolo beguiles all who visit it.

The gardens found their immortality in the spring of 1880, with the unexpected arrival of Richard Wagner, the music world's *wundermeister*. 'Here is the enchanted garden of Klingsor!' he crowed at the sight of voluptuous wisteria vines. He stayed the evening at the villa, banging out the second act of *Parsifal* on an untuned piano, accompanied only by his giant ego and a fierce thunderstorm. After he had played the piano all night long, the music fittingly accented with the lightning bolts of a *tempesta*, the townspeople crowded in

When Sir Francis Neville Reid restored the villa in the 1850s, he embowered the Upper Terrace with immense *pergolati* verdant with oleander, scarlet sage and bougainvillea.

and proclaimed the great composer *pazzo*. They do not call him crazy any longer, though. For the past eighty years, the Villa Rufolo has been the setting for one of Italy's most successful music fêtes, the annual Festivale Musicale di Ravello. Today, the villa's Hall of the Knights often echoes to the sound of Bach, while the Wagner Terrace regularly hosts grand orchestral homages to the composer.

The saga of the villa begins in the late thirteenth century. The Rufolo family owed their riches to trade with Morocco and northern Africa and, in order to court caliphs and kings, they decided to build a residence where they could host lavish feasts in their hometown of Ravello. By this time, Ravello had become the Bel Air of the Amalfi coast, tilting its nose in superiority over its less fashionable neighbours, Atrani and Amalfi, located – pecking-order-wise – further down the hill. By building in the town's ancient cliffside Pendolo quarter, the Rufolos were following patrician Amalfitan families, who, having grown fat and rich on Mediterranean trade, sought to leave the swelting kasbah-like confines of their mother city for *villegiatura* in Ravello's bracing mountaintop air.

By this time, the decorative styles of Morocco and Northern Africa had become the vogue, arriving initially in Sicily in the thirteenth century, then ruled, as Naples was, by the French-Norman court, which had fallen under the Saracenic spell woven by the Muslims who had governed the island for more than two centuries. It was not long before Amalfi – part of the Kingdom of the Two Sicilies – welcomed the decorative twining of Norman medieval and Muslim styles. A trade crossroads, Amalfi, then 'the wealthiest city in the world', also became an artistic crossroads, as its massive cathedral – its Moorish turban-capped belltower appears more minaret than campanile – testifies. The Rufolos themselves had interacted with many Arab merchants, so it is not surprising that they used 'Saracenic' Moorish styles for their villa. Between 1270 and 1280 they created an 'arabo-orientale' extravaganza, a sprawling complex of banqueting halls, pavilions and courtyards, which boasted, as one medieval chronicler put it, 'more rooms than there are days in the year'.

The successful emergence of the Rufolo dynasty owed much to the fortuitous fact of Ravello's high altitude, which kept it safe from Moorish pirates' invasions of the coastal towns. Danger from another source, however, was not so easily avoided. A major conflict was deepening between the Amalfitans and the French-Norman kings, who ruled their Angevin empire from Naples. Closer to home, Ravello's leaders incurred the wrath of the Doge of Amalfi,

Above: Sprays of red oleander brighten the exedra wall of the Upper Terrace. Right: Shade provided by bougainvillea has long invited villa guests – from Boccaccio to Wagner – to linger on the Upper Terrace.

their most powerful neighbour, by siding with the Angevins rather than the Amalfitans, and this led to political and territorial scuffles. The Doge's forces were finally routed in 1086, when a power broker of the Angevin court, Count Roger, using his political connections (do some things never change?) had Ravello named an Angevin bishopric, under the jurisdiction of Pope Victor III. Amalfi had no choice but to accept the ruling of the Church, and with Ravello's independence from Amalfi's power now secure, a grudge was thereby born, collectively expressed by Amalfitans in resentment towards the leading family of Ravello, the Rufolo, and what the Amalfitans saw as their ostentatious excesses.

This staircase, set with planters of scarlet sage, links the Moorish cloister with the Upper Terrace. On the upper parterre stands a rustic trellis.

There may have been grounds to support this view. One legend tells that Charles II was invited to a feast at Marmorata, the Rufolos' coastal harbourage, and that after dinner Rufolo casually but conspicuously tossed the silver platters into the sea (nets having been lowered into the water on the sly to retrieve them). Giovanni Battista Bolvito, writing much later in 1585, tells us that the faience work of winged creatures at the entrance tower to the villa was studded with semi-precious stones. As a result, just as four centuries later the over-the-top *richesse* of the château of Vaux-le-Vicomte made a jealous Louis XIV imprison its creator, his minister of finance, Nicholas Fouquet, so the Villa Rufolo made the Angevin monarchs – the King of Sicily, Charles I, and his crown prince, Charles of Salerno (later Charles II) – see red, or rather green with envy. They turned against the Rufolo family, terminating their friendly ties. The crisis came to a boil in 1283 when, at the urging of Amalfitans incensed by the tax burdens and bullying tactics of the Rufolo family's armoured knights, Charles charged Matteo and Lorenzo Rufolo, father and son, with corruption. They were sentenced to execution (Matteo survived), on which occasion Charles was heard to say, 'To bring seed to harvest a conscientious farmer must frequently rid his fields of thorns.'

Facts such as these were rich fodder for the fertile imagination of Boccaccio in his *Decameron* (1353). In the tale of Day 2, Novelle 4, Boccaccio places a story about one 'Landolfo' Rufolo of Ravello (historians have now determined that he was using the saga of family scion Lorenzo Rufolo) into the mouth of the fair Lauretta. The story tells of a young man 'who, not content with his great store, but anxious to make it double, was near losing all he had, and his life also' and relates how this member of a wealthy and respected family, after losing all his money in a mercantile speculation in Cyprus, turned corsair; was robbed of his new, ill-gotten gains on the high seas, by thievish Genoese merchants; and half-drowned, his arms clasped around a small wooden chest, was rescued off Corfu by a servant-maid. The little chest, of course, was filled with precious stones. With the gems concealed in a belt, the rescued corsair made his way across the Adriatic to the Apulian coast, and reached Ravello with greater wealth than he had left with.

In some of these details, Boccaccio was not straying far from the truth. While the Rufolos had accumulated great wealth serving as bankers-extraordinary to the Angevin kings, their trade activities had increased that wealth a hundredfold. Ships loaded with grain and lumber sailed to such far-flung places as Cordova, Cairo and

Above: Long called the Torre Maggiore, the fourteenth-century Norman campanile of the villa was christened the Wagner Tower after the composer made a celebrated visit in 1880. Right: The columns of the Upper Terrace look down upon the geometric flower beds of the Lower Terrace, the scene of many concerts of the annual Ravello Music Festival.

Constantinople, returning with a cargo of the finest silks and rare spices. Accompanying its rise in stature, before long the family counted four bishops among its members, as well as the banker Matteo Rufolo, whose moneyed arm extended so far as to hold the crown of Charles II of Anjou in pawn. On a roll of pride and privilege, in 1272 Nicolo Rufolo – father to Matteo and grandfather to Lorenzo – had made a gift to Ravello's cathedral of a grand, mosaic-encrusted pulpit and ciborium, which remain among the great medieval treasures of Italy. But, as pride often portends a fall, this act of public munificence was not enough to deter the family's fall from grace, beginning with the charges of corruption, followed by imprisonment, which ended with the execution of Lorenzo.

Thanks to his amour, Maria d'Aquino, daughter of King Robert of Anjou – whom he immortalized in his writings as 'Fiammetta' – Boccaccio had become part of the inner circle of the Neapolitan Angevin court, and, as part of its entourage, travelled to feast at the Villa Rufolo. One can imagine that the French-Normans were both enraptured and scandalized by the villa's sultry splendour, as their own sumptuary laws disdained showy surroundings of the kind the Villa Rufolo revelled in.

But all the Villa Rufolo's kaleidoscopic interlacing of Arab, Sicilian, Byzantine and Norman styles, and its Arabian Nights gorgeousness – the lavish silks and brocades, the tessellated gold and azure domes, the carved-ivory chairs – were but nothing compared to its luxury of luxuries: its verdant garden. In a time and land where water was prized above all things and sold like treasure to the highest bidder, the garden was so vast that it probably needed great porcelain jars in which the forty thieves might have hidden to store water. While the civilizing influences of the Moors had brought many pleasures to Italy – new spices for the banquet table, ikat fabrics for wooden credenzas and new medicines that revolutionized science

Left: A masterpiece of the Arab–Sicilian style of architecture, the fourteenth-century Cortile Moresco (Arab–Sicilian Cloister) seems to echo with the laughter of the Turkish sultans and Angevin kings who once feasted here. The tufa trim is famed for its leaf interlacing and knotting. Right: Majestic cypress trees – yet another element inspired by Arab gardens – frame and dramatize the view across the bay. Overleaf left: Set on gigantic ogival arches, the Norman-style Cavaliers' Hall is another venue for concerts during the summer. Overleaf right: The parterre of the Lower Garden is bedded out with different flowers throughout the year; here it includes geraniums, red begonias and African marigolds (*Tagetes*).

– perhaps their most popular import was the garden, whose origins could be found in the *pairidaeza*, the enclosed parks of the ancient Persian kings. The Villa Rufolo is a prime example of the Muslim 'green revolution' that was so spectacularly allowed to germinate and blossom in Italy and in Spain, where the Alhambra and Generalife gardens in Cordova were laid out by the Moors in the same period. Creating magical contrasts of light and shade, the extensive use of loggias, terraces and patios goes back in time to the modularization of exterior and interior spaces found in Persian gardens.

A slow walk through the garden's mountainside terraces reveals the master plan: a succession of garden rooms, flower parterres, lawns, pools and hedged paths. On the Upper Terrace are expansive stone *pergolati* with hexagonal columns whose upward thrust nicely mirrors soaring cypress trees (which famously hailed from the Persian city of Shiraz). In the Lower Terrace, a vast floral parterre with red, pink and orange flowers is a saturnalia of colour. And everywhere these flowered terraces alternate with Gothic-vaulted halls cool enough to tame the harsh Amalfi sun. This is nowhere more successful than in the villa's famous Cortile Moresco (Arab–Sicilian Cloister). As shadowy as Ali Baba's cave, it seems to echo with the laughter of the Turkish sultans and Angevin kings who once feasted here, no doubt sitting cross-legged on silken pillows while dallying with silk-clad odalisques.

In the middle of the Lower Terrace, evoking the creations of the Moors, who were the architects of countless fountains, pools, dams and aqueducts that still water Sicily and Spain, is set a round pool, in homage to the Islamic *chahar-bagh*, the Persian four-fold garden. This was connected to the enormous irrigation system that fed the garden and which also supplied the thermal baths at the villa – another Muslim grace note. At either side of the circular pool are flower beds whose colours and design conjure up a living Turkish carpet. When it was built, the estate was also covered with magnificent palm trees. Many of these were removed and greatly shortened when the music festival took over, but they still loom large in the Cortile Moresco, where they form part of its celebrated carved stone decoration.

Left: Towering palm trees, medieval columns and thriving coleus act as focal points in the parterre in front of the fourteenth-century arcaded dining room. Right: Ever-changing beds of flowers make the Lower Terrace a feast of colour throughout the year. Overleaf left: At the far end of the dining terrace, beds of touch-me-nots (*Impatiens*) form another seductive corner of the garden. Overleaf right: The Bay of Salerno is rarely out of sight at the villa and reminds us that earthly paradises often come with vistas of water.

Left: Aflame with scarlet sage, a pair of grand staircases links the upper and lower levels of the garden. Above: *Salvia splendens* is also used in various garden parterres.

Today, half medieval cloister, half Aladdin's palace, the Chiostro Moresco wears a relentlessly picturesque face, nearly crumbling and now denuded of its once verdant vegetation. Its forlorn state reminds us that Ravello's glory days were doomed to flicker out, first thanks to Pisa's maritime rise in the fourteenth century, then because of rivalry between its warring families in the fifteenth century and finally when the plague cast its shadow in the seventeenth century. By the time Ravello was incorporated into the diocese of Amalfi in 1804, the population had plummeted from upwards of 30,000 to a few hearty souls, and the Villa Rufolo had become a sleeping beauty.

But as in the fairy tale, a Prince Charming happened upon the villa and kissed it awake in 1851, to bloom again. The princely kiss was bestowed by Sir Francis Neville Reid, Scottish heir to one of Britain's largest breweries; also an amateur archeologist and budding botanist, he was just the person the villa needed. Reid (1826–92) had fallen under the spell of southern Italy during his Grand Tour. After his travels came to an end, he found himself in failing health, and it seemed a good idea to relocate to Naples, which he did in 1845. Establishing a home at the Villa Gallotti – one of the grandest bayside residences of Naples's beautiful Posilipo district – he settled in with his aunt, Lady Mary Gibson-Carmichael, whose husband, Sir Thomas, was a mainstay of Naples's Italo–British colony.

With his health restored, and time and money at his disposal – his wife, Sophie, was a daughter of the well-to-do Sir William Napier – Reid and his wife made their leisurely way south to Amalfi and, intrigued by what they had heard of its unusual scenery, headed to Ravello. Upon learning that the decaying Villa Rufolo was for sale, the couple decided to purchase it from the Marchese d'Afflitto in 1851. In the following years, they set about restoring Ravello's leading patriarchal residence back into a *paradiso*. Before doing so, they decided, in archetypal philanthropic Protestant fashion, to become benefactors to the municipality. They restored Ravello's dilapidated medieval monuments and rebuilt the carriage road from Atrani. Most significantly, they launched a massive irrigation project, which allowed water to flow into Ravello via an aqueduct constructed in 1863, from the nearby hilltop village of Scala. To commemorate the success of this vast undertaking, a fountain was built in the Piazza Vescovada, the town square, which happened to be within splashing distance of the front gates of the Reids' new home. Then began the crash programme of refurbishing the villa, which was placed under the supervision of master craftsman Michele Ruggiero, who later became renowned as leader of the excavations at Pompeii.

Given just a little water, the Villa Rufolo soon blossomed like a rose. The Reids entrusted the gardens to a Ravellese, Luigi Cicalese (1852–1932), father of twelve sons, twenty-six years younger than his employer, an amateur gardener and a passionate photographer (Reid introduced him to the art), who became *capo giardiniere* (head gardener) and ultimately wound up as mayor of Ravello. But Sir Francis remained at the helm throughout the restoration; surviving correspondence between owner and gardener reveals a warm and cooperative relationship.

Being a botanist, Reid always returned from his travels abroad with some example of a rare plant or exotic flower. Interestingly, he made one of his most impressive finds practically next door to the villa: a variety of *Crocus imperati* christened var. *reidii*, a plant with a rose-pink flower indigenous to the Lattari mountains just north of Ravello. Reid realized the need for a herbarium, to complete the garden's encyclopaedic coverage, but he was more interested in the cultivation of rare and exotic plants, which he undertook in the Winter Garden greenhouse. With trees, however, rareness was not a requisite for him: he preferred to select varieties according to their compatibility with his garden ideal. Species still thriving at the villa include *Ginkgo biloba* and palms such as *Phoenix canariensis*. The showpiece is the magnificent *Pinus pinea*, an umbrella pine that, set against the bay and the cupolas of the Santissima Annunziata church, has been enshrined in a million postcards and travel posters.

In reconstructing the Rufolo garden, Reid was at first disappointed to find few remnants of the original estate. But this proved a blessing in disguise, as it gave him free rein to romanticize the form of the new garden as an extrapolation of the Moorish style then back in vogue. This latest theme in nineteenth-century décor, referred to as Orientalism, was illuminated for the public in thousands of oil paintings featuring Turkish harems, smoky Moroccan kasbahs and palm-shaded desert oases – all sensuous images supported by Edward Fitzgerald's *Rubáiyát of Omar Khayyám* (1851). Reid knew that Ravello's climate – both temperate and cultural – would allow some measure of what he intuited his Protestant rector would have pronounced 'gaudiness', but while he attempted to create a *giardino islamico*, or Moorish garden, by filling the Lower Terrace with dazzlingly colourful flowers such as pansies and bergenia, the parterre remains thoroughly Victorianized: it looks not so much like the Alhambra as like the blocks of carpet bedding then fashionable back in England. In his view, Italy's southern gods (not to say balmy climate) deserved – *required* – an incorrigibly romantic and theatrical extravaganza as a worthy subject and he pulled this off so successfully that Richard Wagner was inspired to use the Villa Rufolo garden as the model for a crucial scene in his *Parsifal*.

Having just finished composing the opera, Wagner was looking for inspiration for the production and sets. Depressed by the reign of Bismarck in Germany, he and his wife, Cosima, had decided to become *viaggiatori* in Italy for much of 1880. Arriving in Ravello in January 1880, they spent much of the next seven months residing in Campania's capital – 'Naples is my city,' Wagner once wrote. Three days after the composer's sixty-seventh birthday, he, Cosima

and the composer's close friend, the Russian–German set designer Baron Paul von Joukowsky, set out by train from Naples for Amalfi. Cosima's *Tagebücher* for 26 May 1880 reveals that 'after a gay breakfast' they rode up to Ravello, 'beautiful beyond words'. After lunch at the town's Hotel Palumbo (Richard and Cosima took a fancy to the owner's Swiss wife), they toured the Villa Rufolo, where Wagner promptly fell under its picturesquely medieval spell. Exotic and voluptuously perfumed, the garden was just the setting he was looking for, for Klingsor's Garden. When he saw von Joukowsky's sketches of the garden, done *en plein air*, he offered the set designer the commission to do *Parsifal* on the spot. Ecstatic at his discovery, Wagner inscribed '*Klingsor's zauber Garden ist gefunden*' (Here is the enchanted garden of Klingsor) in the Hotel Palumbo's guest book (where his signature takes up half the page). The following day, the party left for Naples where, according to Frau Wagner, 'Vesuvius, as if to celebrate our return, gushes sparks in the evening.' In the première of *Parsifal* in July 1882 at Bayreuth, the Rufolo garden was recreated on stage.

If Klingsor proved top wizard for Parsifal, the real magician at the Villa Rufolo turned out to be Luigi Cicalese, who had transformed, to quote Wagner, 'this *deserto* into a *giardino di delizie*,' and all this wrought in the years since Reid's purchase in 1851. Richard and Cosima would, no doubt, be delighted to see that the Villa Rufolo blooms as luxuriantly as ever today, thanks to a team of gardeners supervised by the villa's director, Dr Secondo Amalfitano. Related to the last descendants of the Cicalese gardening dynasty, Vincenzo and Giovanni – both startlingly young – are now the main gardeners for the vast estate.

They superintend the garden's two main plantings every year: April/May for flowering annuals, September/October for other plants (although other blooms that can resist colder climes, like cyclamen, geraniums and begonia, are also planted then to provide colour throughout the year). The gardeners' coaxing digits are never stilled and they are constantly looking for ways to improve the grounds. For instance, in 2008 they altered the entryway allée to the garden, which, with its enormously tall oak trees and Norman tower, had long been a shadowed area. Now, having cut back the tree

Begonias grow on the villa's medieval walls and bring their light and colour to the garden on even the gloomiest days.

branches to allow sun to penetrate, they have lined the main entry pathway with radiantly colourful pansies. No longer is Reid's Winter Garden greenhouse needed to nuture new plants, as many – exotics as well as indigenous – are now bought directly from suppliers, who are happy to provide them as a means of sponsorship for the Villa Rufolo. Their help is greatly appreciated: after all, one parterre alone comprises more than 1,700 plants.

Today, the fantastic 'arabo-orientale' flavour of the garden, the soaring Norman tower (now called the Wagner Tower), the pergolas smothered in bougainvillea and the incomparable vista over the azure Bay of Salerno all together conspire to make this one of the most magical settings in Italy. Part medieval, part Moorish, the Villa Rufolo is the most spectacular agglomeration of Latin and Islamic motifs on the Amalfi coast, a collision of Orientalism and Romanticism that makes a *deliziosissimo* setting for Ravello's music festival. Whether visitors choose to hum along with Placido, attend a *concerto di alba* (to watch the sun come up at 4.00 a.m. with orchestral accompaniment) or listen to Wagner echoing off the medieval tower, for them a chorus of 'My Blue Heaven' will undoubtedly prove to be the perfect encore.

Shading the twin cupolas of the thirteenth-century church of
Santissima Annunziata, this umbrella or stone pine (*Pinus pinea*)
is the hero of a thousand travel posters and perhaps the most beloved
umbrella pine in the world.

Garbo's Shangri-La
Villa Cimbrone
Ravello

Once upon a time, Ravello ranked as the quietest town in the world, so naturally Greta Garbo showed up. But, for once, she did not want to be alone. The Aloof Goddess arrived at the impossibly beautiful fishing village perched 1,500 feet/460 metres upon a flank of Monte Cerreto in 1938 in the company of the conductor and Hollywood luminary Leopold Stokowski, eager to enjoy *cavalleria rusticana* on a glamorous scale. Dizzily suspended between earth and heaven over the blue Bay of Salerno in the Tyrhennian Sea, 'closer to the sky than the sea', as André Gide had put it, '*la città più tranquilla, solitaria, e silenziosa*' was a little world unto itself. Sociable even in its silences, La Bellissima (The Most Beautiful), as the town was nicknamed, had been blessed with a delicious sense of solitude, far removed from the touristic conveyor belt then beginning to hum along the shores of the Amalfi coast. A fortress of quiet, Ravello had become a favoured sanctuary for artists, writers, musicians and wealthy *Inglesi*, all of whom loved the idea that there was even something *sotto voce* in the town's crowded grand hotels. It was a retreat perfectly tailored for Garboian evasiveness.

Or so Garbo and Stokowski thought. A week after their arrival on 25 February at the town's most noted residence, the Villa Cimbrone – which they had rented for a month from its owner, Lord Grimthorpe, who had built it as an escape from the formalities of English court life – the stop-the-presses word leaked to a thoroughly unexpectant world that the twosome had been spotted enjoying meals at the town's Hotel Caruso-Belvedere. Their casual 'friendship' quickly developed into a hectic bit of headline material. Ever since Stokowski's American wife had divorced him the December before, Tinseltown gossips had been kept on tiptoe. Half of Hollywood was placing bets that a marriage was imminent,

This parterre between the Rose Terrace and the Viale dell'Immensità is set with statues of two Greek wrestlers, Damosseno and Greucante, each surrounded by beds bright with white and red begonias.

and now all the signs suggested that La Garbo was on the point of committing to matrimony. Ravello was promptly invaded by an army of reporters. The articles they filed managed to knock coverage of events that were to lead to the worst war the world had ever seen off front pages everywhere.

With the identity of Ravello's 'Donna Misteriosa' established, *Time* magazine reported on 14 March that the couple were 'trying not to notice that all the world was watching them'. Having raised a few million eyebrows worldwide – as *Time* continued, 'romantic villagers were clacking of arm-in-arm walks in twilight, unabashed embraces' – and besieged by the press, after three weeks the couple finally consented to giving a press conference, in order to prove there were no secrets to hide. Sitting in a blue gabardine suit, yellow sweater and blue scarf, the chicly bobbed aristocrat of the silver screen confessed to reporters gathered in the library of the Villa Cimbrone that she was just out for the ride: 'Miss Garbo said she was so alarmed by "cruel events happening in the world today" that she thought its beauty might not last much longer and she wanted to see it before it vanished,' according to the *New York Times*.

Above: In previous years some statues were surrounded by species from the Rose Terrace, in particular the 'Rose of Ravello', a rare hybrid with five petals created in the 1920s by Viscountess Frost, daughter of the one-time owner Lord Grimthorpe. Overleaf: Surrounding the rose garden is a green parterre shadowed by umbrella pines and set with four classical statues – two ancient athletes and Flora, goddess of Spring, and Leda and the Swan – along with a giant urn.

If, as the magazines all predicted, the star was thinking about giving up her life of 'solitary confinement', what more romantic setting than the Villa Cimbrone could sway her? More evocative of the pages of Gabriele d'Annunzio's *Francesca da Rimini* than the tabloid love affair reported breathlessly by *Modern Screen*, the achingly beautiful Villa Cimbrone was designed for courtly love. It had a vast garden that lent itself to confidences. Its Belvedere of Infinity was just the place for an immortal screen goddess to do her callisthenics.

It had a privacy and calm unchallenged by a braying press. A sublime oasis, it was known to its many guests – among them King Alfonso VII, D.H. Lawrence, Coco Chanel, the Duke and Duchess of Kent and Winston Churchill – as the jewel in Ravello's crown.

Legend has it that Ravello was founded by ancient Romans who, shipwrecked by a storm on the coast, took sanctuary in the hills above Amalfi and called the location *res bella* (a beautiful place). The town enjoyed its golden age in the thirteenth century, when it became a retreat for wealthy families from nearby Amalfi, who, newly rich from trade with Constantinople, built enormous estates in the secluded village. Because of Ravello's secluded setting, these medieval structures remained practically untouched until the nineteenth century, when a stream of aristocratic Englishmen arrived to wake up the slumbering town.

After the Amalfi Drive's Strada Esmeralda highway was built in 1853 by Ferdinand, King of the Two Sicilies, a host of glitterati – among them Wagner, the Duchess of Devonshire and Grieg – discovered the wonders of the Amalfi coast, including Ravello, with its perfectly tonsured palm trees and gardens out of the Arabian Nights, its pastel palazzi, tucked-away piazzas with medieval fountains, architecture ranging from Romano–Byzantine to Norman–Saracen and the most sumptuous blue-water, blue-sky vistas in the world. Like a monastery without confinement, Ravello acted like catnip to a host of literati: Virginia Woolf, E.M. Forster, Vita Sackville-West, D.H. Lawrence, Graham Greene, Tennessee Williams and Gore Vidal all came here to work on their books.

Southern Italy worked on English tight-laced inhibitions like four glasses of *vino bianco*. And no one appreciated this more than Ernest William Beckett, the 2nd Lord Grimthorpe (1856–1917), a rich banker whose family had a distinguished past in Yorkshire. Nurtured by the Aesthetic movement, he had become a passionate humanist with a love for art, beauty and the antiquarian past. While he became partner in the family's banking firm of Beckett & Co. of Leeds, and was elected to represent Whitby in Parliament (a seat he held until 1905), he had a profound enthusiasm not just for the arts but also for everyday living. His life was one of nearly Maecenean splendour; no matter that he gambled incessantly in Monte Carlo – he was reputed to have an infallible system of his own devising for playing roulette – or that his family fortune took a big hit after his trustees invested money in San Francisco just before the city was struck by the mammoth 1906 earthquake.

With the tastes and manners of a Renaissance lord, he associated with artists and poets, spending many of his days travelling from one princely house in France and Italy to another. On one of these trips, he visited Ravello – newly fashionable to wealthy *Inglesi* – and was smitten. Upon returning to England, chance would have it that he met Nicolo Mansi, a Ravellese who, like many of his compatriots, had travelled to England to find employment (he had been trained as a tailor). Beckett took him for a kindred spirit and, more importantly, a soul who evinced a style that was intensely Amalfitan. When Mansi learned that Ravello's most famous estate might be for sale, he recommended that Ernest Beckett return to Ravello and investigate; and, in 1904, Beckett purchased the town's fabled promontory, the Cimbronium. Like so many other foreigners who had created gardens in this region, he had fallen under the 'incantesimo solare' (enchantment of the sun), to use d'Annunzio's phrase.

The estate had existed for hundreds, perhaps thousands, of years. Giorgio Vuillemier, whose family now owns the estate and has transformed it into one of the most beautiful hotels in Italy, has dug deep into its history and unearthed new information about its earliest owners, beginning with ancient Roman landlords. Cimbrone has, in fact, been known as a celebrated spot ever since the days of the Romans, who planted extensive vineyards in this region and felled many of the trees in the forests here for the construction of boats. Called *cimber*, these trees gave the estate its name, Cimbronium.

When the new rich of the region built extensive estates here in the twelfth and thirteenth centuries, the great Fusco family, related to the rich d'Angio family of Naples, purchased the estate from the Acconciajoco clan and settled in for an ownership of more than 500 years. There was a reason the Fuscos needed to set down roots: a family member had recently been appointed Bishop of Ravello. The Fusci remade the Cimbrone into the showpiece of the Borgata Santa Chiara, the southernmost district of Ravello landmarked by the thirteenth-century convent of Santa Chiara and patronized by Cardinal Della Rovere (whose papal coat of arms once graced the Cimbrone's main entrance).

The Fusco years were happy ones for the villa, culminating in the years 1620 to 1800, when the family constructed what is now known as the Belvedere of Infinity, the great stone terrace that overlooks the sea, magnificently ornamented with six stone busts *di fantasia* sculpted in the outré seventeenth-century Neapolitan Baroque style. By this point, the Fuscos had gilded their family tree by marrying into the Pitti family of Florence and the Cimbrone's aesthetic connection with *lo stile Fiorentino* begins here. One of the Fusco chatelaines

– a signora named Isabella del Verme Sasso – undertook a grand renovation of the Cimbrone, adding salons replete with frescoed ceilings inspired by those of the Pitti Palace. This halcyon era, however, came to an abrupt end in the early 1800s, when Naples was beset by the conquering forces of the French. With the Neapolitan family seat in chaos, the Fusci forgot about their far-flung country estate and the Cimbrone sank into obscurity.

With Ravello's renaissance in the mid-nineteenth century, however, the Cimbrone was bought by the Amici family. The estate ultimately descended to two sisters, who, warring with each other, decided to split it between them, one retaining the land overlooking the sea, the other claiming the land overlooking the Vallone dei Dragone (Valley of the Dragon), using the town road (today the villa's long Viale dell'Immensità) as a dividing marker. They also constructed a wall in the house itself, sub-dividing it into two abodes. It was when one of these *sorelle* decided to sell that Nicolo

Mansi tipped off Ernest Beckett, who, in 1904, purchased one half of the estate; five years later, he acquired the other half from the other sister.

While nature had given the villa a marvellous site, genius was needed to take advantage of all the resources of art and wealth and transform it. It took Lord Grimthorpe twelve years to accomplish the miracle of converting the savage cliff into an eden of enchantment. From 1904 to his death in 1916, he laid out the extensive, 12-acre/

Opposite: The former badminton court was transformed into the Rose Terrace – from May to October blooming with and perfumed by an array of French and English roses – by Viscountess Frost with much help from her friend Vita Sackville-West. The balustrade covered in Moorish-style tilework provides the perfect frame for the 'carpet' of roses created by the garden's gravel paths and quadrant rose beds. Below left: Potted coleuses flank the main doorway to the villa. Below right: The Music Room, one of the villa's salons.

5-hectare garden and built a new villa in which to house his wife Diana, daughter Lucy and son Ralph, along with a vast array of acquaintances, most notably *le tout Bloomsbury*, who had been introduced to the estate by Beckett's reputed illegitimate daughter, the novelist Violet Trefusis, whose visits to the Cimbrone included one in 1914, with her then-amour, the novelist and garden authority Vita Sackville-West. Violet was very much her father's daughter, if her love of gardens and Italy are proof. She wrote novels about Florentine playboys (*Pirates at Play*), resided with her mother Alice Keppel (mistress of Edward VII) at the magnificent Fiesole estate of L'Ombrellino and was fond of exclaiming *'Bisogna begonia!'*

When Lord Grimthorpe set out to beautify his Italian estate, he would probably have been inspired by the gardening books of the day – among them H. Inigo Triggs's *The Art of Garden Design in Italy* (1906), George S. Elgood's *Italian Gardens* (1907), Charles A. Platt's *Italian Gardens* (1904), Edith Wharton's *Italian Villas and their Gardens* (1904), and Sir Reginald Blomfield's *The Formal Garden in England* (1892). More esoteric literary sources – the *novellini* of Boccaccio, the stanzas of d'Annunzio, Maurice Barres's *Amori et dolori sacrum* – also coloured his vision: his copies of these books are still retained in the villa's library and they were put to good use by his eldest daughter, Lucy.

While Nicolo Mansi was delegated major-domo for construction and the estate's aesthetic renovation was mainly overseen by Beckett himself, the lord delegated the refurbishment and redesign of the gardens to his beloved 'Lucilla'. Whatever her training, or lack of it, she wound up creating a garden that was a tradition-breaker. Historians now believe that a good deal of her wizardry was achieved with the help of Vita Sackville-West's advice, given on her visit and through correspondence.

As for the villa itself, Beckett envisioned a romantic castello-palazzo *a la* d'Annunzio. Unlike his uncle, the 1st Lord Grimthorpe, who was most famous for designing the casement for London's Big Ben but was also one of England's most castigated gentlemen-architects (responsible for the restoration of St Albans Cathedral with additions so controversial that the verb 'to grimthorpe' came into popular usage to describe unsympathetic restorations of historic structures), Beckett managed to envision a medievalized castle entirely *rispettoso* to its surroundings. It was, in fact, an architectural homage to that medieval aficionado Richard Wagner and his historic 1880 visit to Ravello.

With a *torre di difesa* (defensive tower), Beckett's villa flaunted a Saracenic cloister inspired by the one at the Convento di San Francesco just down the hill; a neo-Gothic crypt modelled on the one at Fountains Abbey (near the ancestral home of the Beckett family in Malton, in Yorkshire); and another tower, inspired by the crumbling Byzantine campanile of Ravello's San Martino. Storybook battlements, carved pillars, Moorish trims and bifurcated ogival windows worthy of an ancient Venetian palace were also added – making the villa the quintessence of romantic antiquarianism. Inside, the décor was a pageant of *fin-de-siècle* historicism. Raphael-style *grotteschi* frescoed ceilings, medieval tapestries, 'Gothic' lecterns, antique bronzes, Castel Durante majolica and Savonarola chairs fit for a Florentine cardinal all created an *ambiente rinascimentale*.

The villa's homage to the Renaissance was meant to evoke the Fusco family and their connections with the Florentine Pitti. In view of these Tuscan antecedents, it is not inappropriate to think that Beckett also looked at examples of Medici feudal architecture; at once fortresses and cultivated retreats, the Medici estates of Il Trebbio, Cafaggiolo and Careggi may have provided inspiration for his castle. Thus Beckett, whose ancestral pedigree was recent (he was but the second baron of one of England's newest titles, bestowed on the 1st Lord as lately as 1872), rooted his home in the past.

Enlivened by whimsy, the Cimbrone garden is the apotheosis of the romantic, picturesque garden. Its 'spine' is the Viale dell'Immensità (Street of Immensity), a ruler-straight, 1,640-foot/500-metre-long walk that follows the centuries-old Stradare dei Fusco but transforms it into a magnificent promenade shaded by cypress, acacia and arbutus, and lined with ancient pots and plinths. The Viale leads promenaders under the Renaissance-inspired Ponte del Rosea, a bridge over which grow cascades of roses and, in May, a purple mist of overhanging wisteria. You emerge from the shade of the bridge – which connects two separate gardens on either side of the Viale – into the sparkle of sunlight. This is the first of many such contrasts of light and dark which have a powerful impact, the effect of surprise and suggestiveness being important in this garden. The Viale lends a strong north–south axis to the park, but on either side the grounds are full of crosswalks that divide and conquer the estate into hidden 'islands' – many so shrouded in verdant privacy that you hardly know the next one is there – where unexpected discovery is one of the greatest delights.

Geraniums brighten the fountain near the entrance to the Villa Cimbrone. The villa's neo-Gothic *torre di difensa* (defensive tower) was inspired by Wagner's visit to the villa in 1880.

To the east of the Viale, however, the eye is greeted by the estate's one open space, a wide 'English' lawn that is framed with Japanese cherry trees, multicoloured hortensia and antique-inspired statues representing Greek warriors. At the sides, towering *Pinus pinea* finger the air while other trees, including *Platanus orientalis,* beguile the eye. Adding still more variety are statues of four dancers, ancient topiary and century-old pots. In contrast, the gardens that lie on the western side of the Viale dell' Immensità are almost withheld from view, playing hide and seek not only from the stroller but from each other. While the temptation is to explore these gardens and meander like a butterfly from side to side, the Viale all but demands you promenade directly to the garden's famous showpiece, the Terrazza dell'Infinito, or the Terrace of Infinity.

From this spectacular castle in the air an infinite, clear, blue Campanian sky presents a sight for which the appellation 'stupendous' seems too mean a term. Stepping on to this rocky crest of Ravello has been likened to the effect of drinking a spiritual cocktail made of equal parts mirage, paradise and Shangri-La. Study the incomparable vista and you'll understand that the celestial blue

Opposite: A detail of the ivy-covered Saracenic Cloister, inspired by one at the nearby Convento di San Francesco; filled with an array of medieval sculptures, it is brightened by planters filled with petunias and begonias. Above left: Hydrangeas provide spots of colour on a hillock diademed with Lord Grimthorpe's Moorish-style Tea Pavilion. Above right: The gardens are home to an array of ornamental statues, such as this copy of Donatello's *David*. Overleaf left and right: Found at the end of an *allée* of cypress tress and lavender hedges is the Temple of Bacchus, a *tempietto* built of Vesuvian stone which looks out over the Valley of the Dragon. The cupola bears the famed aphorism by Catallus: '*O quid solutis est beatius curis cum mens onus reponit ac peregrino labore fessi venimus larem ad nostrum desiteratoque acquiescimus lecto*' (The most beautiful thing is when, after having finished our work, with the spirit free from any worry and tired because of the labour carried out for others, we return to our houses and we lie down to rest on the cherished bed we so desire). The quote is apt, for, beneath the reproduction of the ancient bronze statue of the *Bacchus,* the ashes of Lord Grimthorpe have found their final resting place under the pedestal.

is not a colour but more like a miracle. The stone balcony, restored by Lord Grimthorpe in 1907, commands one of the most sublime prospects: the entire Bay of Salerno, from Ravello all the way to the Cilento mountains and the ancient plains of Paestum, home of the fabled Greek temples.

The Cimbrone's spectacular *balconata belvedere* is ingeniously built on to the outermost ridge of the promontory, sitting so high above the Bay of Salerno that it might be poised for a dive. They say that every English garden is in search of a view, and here Lord Grimthorpe had the Amalfi coast's most gasp-inducing one. Before you a veil of celestial blue extends as far as the eye can see; and because you can't tell where the blue sea ends and the sky begins, the view is nothing less than an invitation into the beyond. D'Annunzio famously proclaimed this was the one spot you could be 'embraced by the arms of Infinity'.

As visitors stand gazing in wonder at the endless waters of the

Tyrrhenian sea below they are not alone: the parapet is adorned with eight busts of Renaissance courtesans and *condottieri*, which punctuate the panorama like eight sculpted exclamation points. Now lichen-covered and stained moss agate, they seem ancient but actually are eighteenth-century Neapolitan *opere di fantasia*. Here, a general seems to wink at you with amusement; there, a donna leans forward, as if to hear the latest gossip, with eyes that imply 'Tell me all.' They have an air of baroque grotesquerie that expresses Lord Grimthorpe's *folletto*, or tricksy spirit.

When Beckett restored the centuries-old belvedere in 1910, he also restored the Doric *tempietto* that is silhouetted against the sky at the end of the Viale dell'Immensità and forms a gateway to the terrace. Under its cupola, Lord Grimthorpe set a nineteenth-century reproduction of a statue of Ceres, the goddess of harvest, agriculture and *civiltà* (the original is in the Galleria Borghese in Rome).

The long Viale was perfect for cooler days when the sun warmed

strollers, but in the heat of a Campanian afternoon, cool, shady walks were also needed and the eastern flank of the Cimbrone estate was given over to these. They begin to the left of Ceres's Doric temple, where a path running past the Belvedere café descends to a grassy sward inset with a mound of flowering hydrangeas – an elegant repoussage to a veritable forest of chestnuts and oaks which looms in the distance, with *Rhododendron ponticum* (at their most southerly sea-level station in Italy) beckoning in mysterious luxuriance. Like a sacred wood, these groves conjure up the late nineteenth-century poems of d'Annunzio, which sketched the love affairs of fauns in moonlit forests.

From here, a flight of stone steps leads you past a hedge of hebes encircled by giant arbutus to a rocky escarpment, the Seat of Mercury. Overlooking a stupendous view of the Vallone dei Dragone and reposing upon a boulder is a fine eighteenth-century bronze reproduction of *Resting Mercury*, sculpted by the School of Lysippus

Left: The high point, literally and figuratively, of most visitors' trips to the Amalfi coast is the Villa Cimbrone's famous Terrazza dell'Infinito, or Terrace of Infinity, the only place d'Annunzio said, where you can be 'embraced by the arms of infinity'. Entirely restored by Lord Grimthorpe in 1907, this *balconata belvedere* is believed to have existed ever since the days of ancient Rome. Above: A statue of the goddess Ceres ornaments the Doric *tempietto* that Lord Grimthorpe constructed at the end of the Viale dell'Immensità.

Above: Overlooking the sea, a copy of Lysippus's famed
Mercury Resting crowns the Poggio di Mercurio belvedere.
Right: A view down the spine of the garden, the Viale
dell'Immensità, 1,640 feet/500 metres long, to the Temple
of Ceres – nicknamed 'the doorway to the Sun' – which leads
to the Terrace of Infinity. The *allée*, bordered by holm oaks
and exotica such as sughera, also passes under a stone pergola
which is spectacularly covered with purple and white wisteria
in season. Opposite: one of the seven delightful Neapolitan
figura di fantasia that adorn the Belvedere of Infinity.

(now at Naples's Museo Nazionale Archeologico). On the cliffside, a plaque bears a verse composed in 1927 by one of the villa's most celebrated guests, D.H. Lawrence:

> Lost to a world in which I crave no part
> I sit alone and commune with my heart
> Pleased with my little corner of the earth
> Glad that I came not sorry to depart.

In places nearly ethereal, this garden is also intensely human, as the many stanzas, inscriptions and poems Lord Grimthorpe and his children had engraved and set on walls and along paths prove. Their leitmotif is sounded by the verse of Terence near the base of the villa's tower, which you read as you enter the grounds: '*Humani Nil A Me Alienum Puto*' (Nothing that is human is alien to me). The quotations scattered through the gardens may be by several writers but the poet is just one: Lord Grimthorpe.

The path overlooking the Vallone dei Dragone soon deposits you at the foot of an avenue lined with cypresses, an allée of trysting trees, accented with hedges of lavender, that leads majestically to the Temple of Bacchus. This *tempietto* of eight Doric columns in Vesuvian stone is topped by an impressive cupola, on whose trabeation is set a stanza of Catullus extolling the virtues of home: 'The most beautiful thing is when after having finished our work, with the spirit free from any worry and tired because of the labour carried out for others, we return to our houses and we lie down to rest on the cherished bed.' In this case, the 'bed' refers to Lord Grimthorpe's final resting place, for his ashes are buried beneath the pedestal, which bears a copy of the School of Praxiteles's *Dionysius* (from the Museo Nazionale in Naples). A bronze full-length satyr holds a bacchic infant on his shoulder and a bunch of grapes in his hand, and leans for support against a tree wrapped with vine shoots and adorned with Pan pipes, the instrument used for orgiastic dances back in the ancient days of myth.

From here, a path passes a natural cavern known as Eve's Grotto, where a statue by Tadolini, student of Canova, represents the mother of mankind. Seen naked on a mound of fig leaves, she is carved in

One of the seven busts of Renaissance courtesans and *condottieri* which punctuate the Terrace of Infinity's panorama like sculpted exclamation points. Now lichen-covered and stained moss agate, they seem ancient but in fact were fashioned by an eighteenth-century Neapolitan sculptor.

a translucent marble that radiates an almost flesh-like glow when hit by the rays of the setting sun. A wisteria-draped walkway then leads you up the hillside to a ridge with a fantastical rock garden and an impressive columned pergola bearing Banksia roses and with hydrangeas planted underneath, which imitates the famous Medici pergola at Il Trebbio. The Florentine motif is underscored by the reproduction by the nineteenth-century Neapolitan sculptor Gioacchino Varlese of Verrocchio's *David*, which is on view at the Bargello.

The dark, cool *bosco* follows the natural earthen staircase up the hill and then gives way to the Rose Terrace on the site of the estate's badminton court. Set within a fantastical balustrade of Arab–Sicilian style inset with coloured tiling, four beds lined with terracotta trefoil piping create a pattern that conjures up nothing so much as an Islamic carpet (a Saracenic motif perhaps inspired by the style of the neighbouring Villa Rufolo). Here, with Victorian over-abundance, Lucy Beckett planted hundreds of standard rose varieties. Together with the rose parterres outside the balustrade – gorgeously adorned with antique statues, giant urns and towering cypresses – the profusion of blooms seems more English than Italian. Not a professional gardener, Lucy had much recourse to Gertrude Jekyll's 1902 *Roses for English Gardens* and William Robinson's 1883 *The English Flower Garden*, along with first-hand advice and information provided by Vita Sackville-West.

Within the balustrade, every rose is staked, tied, trained and identified, the most famous being the 'Rose of Ravello', a rare hybrid of five petals created by Lucy in the 1930s for a San Remo contest. The rosary is at its most flowerful in June, but it has been planted with a wide range of varieties so that roses colour the garden and scent the air throughout the year. By this decade, Lucy had married Manfred, Viscount Frost, and later Viscount and Viscountess Frost created their own home by transforming an old chapel perched just below the Villa Cimbrone and enjoying a spectacular toehold on a cliff over the Bay of Salerno. For decades the residence of the author Gore Vidal, La Rondinaia (The Swallow's Nest) was purchased by a luxury hotelier in 2006.

The sense of cultivated beauty continues past an ivied wall into the Tea Room, a neo-Byzantine pavilion where afternoon teas were held. An inscription carved above an antique wall basin – 'Scatter roses: I hate the hands that will not scatter' – reminds us that the geometric beds here were once planted with roses; now they bloom with pansies and begonias. Bedded-out parterres are rare in southern Italy, but these tip their hat to those at the Villa Rufolo, which is also conjured up in the pavilion, for its right-hand exterior wall mirrors the Saracenic ornament of the Rufolo's Moorish courtyard. With, too, Arabo-Sicilian columns, an archway that echoes Florence's Pazzi Chapel, an English twelfth-century baptismal well and four chiselled Byzantine columns (one of the largest colonies of foreigners in Constantinople were Amalfitans), this setpiece, nothing if not eclectic, concludes the garden tour on a note of whimsical formality.

As garden historian Charles Quest-Riston noted in *The English Garden Abroad*, 'The Italian influence [here] is strong, although the gardens could only have been made by an Englishman.' Emphatically Amalfitan by adoption, Lord Grimthorpe was at heart a northern European and his garden is an eccentric extravaganza that is Italian at base but covered with a *sauce anglaise*. As you walk through it and trace Lord Grimthorpe's labour of love, you realize that he used the clarity and order of the Renaissance as a bridge to unify the modernity of Romanticism with the Rome of antiquity. In the end, Lord Grimthorpe was content to throw out the connoisseurship of the archaeologist and create a garden that, compelling in its dramatic impact, remains an unforgettable landmark of English exoticism.

The Bay of Salerno seen from the Terrace of Infinity's interior, which was once fitted out with a kitchen for Lord Grimthorpe's terrace parties and is now home to the hotel's small *caffé*.

Amalfi con Amore

Il Santa Caterina

Amalfi

*Y*our first whiff of *profumo della terra*, a head-clearing blast of sun-warmed pinewoods and delicate gentia, stops you in your tracks. Better get used to it: you're safe and secure in the garden of the Hotel Santa Caterina, set far from the crowds of Amalfi. An island of quiet, this idyllic estate blankets an entire hillside. An uncut emerald of green, it quickly shifts stressed nervous systems into neutral. One day here and you feel thoroughly Edenized.

No wonder Elizabeth Taylor and Richard Burton escaped here from the vast posse of paparazzi plaguing their final scene in *Cleopatra* – the Queen of the Nile's entry on her gilded barge – on Ischia. They discovered the hotel to be a heaven of solitude, thanks to a vast park that kept the outer world at bay. What better place than this charmingly secluded retreat to continue their epic love affair?

So seductive was the setting that the duo chose to have their lunches alfresco instead of in the dining room. According to Carmela Gambardella, whose family has owned the property since 1850, 'They were a wonderful couple, but lively and often quarrelled,' she reminisces. 'But after such spats they wound up taking long walks through the garden and always returned in a tender embrace.' The serpent in their paradise was time: they stayed only four days.

Today, the garden remains a landscape for lovers. Jasmine, bougainvillea, and strelitzia enchant the eye, but a walk through the grounds also reveals a gigantic orchard, with separate terraces given over to olive groves, lemon and orange trees, and enfilades of vegetables. Figs, apricots, peaches, rocket, lettuce, tomatoes, courgettes, peppers, aubergines, artichokes and pumpkins all garnish dishes in the hotel's celebrated restaurant.

While these incredible edibles are the last word in sustainability, they also underscore the fact that gardens on the Amalfi coast began as farms, terraced with *macere* (containment walls) and often planted with lemons, first brought west by Alexander the Great's armies from Hesperia and then cultivated by Italy's Moorish conquerors. By the days of the Caesars, Campania was known as the vegetable patch of the Roman Empire, partly due to the *terra pulla* – the immensely fertile black volcanic soil stirred up by Vesuvius – that covered parts of the province. Goethe, in his *Italian Journey*, notes: 'Here the soil produces everything, and one can expect three to five harvests a year . . . the fields are worked on till they are as smooth and tidy as garden beds.' Citriculture still takes pride of place here, as the coast's famed limoncello attests. At the Santa Caterina lemons – 'Sfusato Amalfitano' – as big as oranges are grown in both the oval and 'nippled' shapes. One soufflé made with them here and you realize that Amalfi is a slice of edible paradise.

The Santa Caterina continues to offer what Signora Gambardella calls a '*cielo della quieta*', quoting Dante. And it still must work its witchery, at least for Angelina Jolie and Brad Pitt. Newspapers reported that when the couple stayed here while filming *Mr And Mrs Smith* (2005) the Hollywood diva was initially ensconced in the garden's historic hunting-box chalet, with Pitt holed up in a grand hotel suite. But every afternoon they began to enjoy a garden rendezvous. Before long, love was in bloom, right along with the verdant beds of passionflower.

It is easy to see why the Santa Caterina has been such a love nest during its distinguished history: the surroundings here are pretty to the point of giddiness. Little wonder one guest wrote '*Veni. Vidi. Amore*' in the hotel's *libro d'oro*. Indeed, prospective grooms often stay here for the sole purpose of proposing, for in such a setting, even frog-princelings look like princes. The enchanting landscape of this garden accounts for a good deal of the hotel's allure. To fully savour the show, pull up a chair by the garden's bougainvillea 'window' and enjoy a view so picturesque it practically drips off the canvas. The vista stretches out to the liquid horizon, with Amalfi shining brightly under the *mezzogiornale* sun. As you let the tranquillity of this garden surround you, you soon forget your problems and the headlines, and know you will never forget beauty and peace.

Near the hotel's nineteenth-century waterside chalet, this view through a bougainvillea 'window' extends to the entrance of Amalfi's harbour.

Visiting the Gardens

While many of the gardens in this book are private, there are others that are open to the public for visits and, in the case of the hotel gardens included, actual stays. For up-to-date visiting information and opening times, visit the gardens' websites or telephone them.

Cloistered Charms
Santa Chiara (Chiostro delle Clarisse)
Via Santa Chiara 49/c
Spaccanapoli District, Naples
Tel: 081 5516673
www.santachiara.info

I Girolamini
Via Duomo 142
Spaccanapoli District, Naples
Tel: 331 4267722

The Good Volcano
Palazzo Reale, Orto Botanico (Giardino della Regina)
Via Universita 100
Portici (5km south-east of Naples)
Tel: 081 7755136
www.museiagraria.unina.it
By appointment

When Knighthood Was in Flower
Castello Lancellotti (Associazione Pro Lauro)
Piazza Castello Città Lauro
Lauro (Avellino, 40km south-east of Naples)
Tel: 081 8240013
www.castellolancelotti.it/; www.prolauro.it

The Global Garden
Orto Botanico di Napoli
Via Foria 223
Naples
Tel: 081 449759
www.ortobotanico.unina.it
By appointment

Seeds of Inspiration
La Mortella
Via Francesco Calise 39
Ischia (42km east of Naples)
Tel: 081 986220
www.lamortella.org

It Has Been a Beautiful Day
Villa San Michele
Viale Axel Munthe 34
Anacapri
Capri (46km south of Naples)
Tel: 081 8371401
www.villasanmichele.eu

The Island Way
Hotel La Certosella
Via Tragara 13
Capri (46km south of Naples)
Tel: 081 8784644
www.hotelcertosella.com

A Regal Realm
Hotel Parco dei Principi
Via Rota 1
Sorrento (43km south-east of Naples)
Tel: 081 8370713
www.grandhotelparcodeiprincipi.net

La Dolce Vista
Hotel Il San Pietro
Via Laurito 2
Positano (53km south-east of Naples)
Tel: 089 875455
www.ilsanpietro.it

Blossom Fever
Hotel Palazzo Murat
Via dei Mulini 23
Positano (53km south-east of Naples)
Tel: 089 875177
www.palazzomurat.it

The Flower and the Glory
Villa Rufolo
Piazza Duomo
Ravello (65km south-east of Naples)
Tel: 089 857621
www.villarufolo.it

Garbo's Shangri-La
Hotel Villa Cimbrone
Via Santa Chiara 26
Ravello (65km south-east of Naples)
Tel: 089 857459
www.villacimbrone.com

Amalfi con Amore
Hotel Santa Caterina
Strada Amalfitana 9
Amalfi (62km south-east of Naples)
Tel: 089 871012
www.hotelsantacaterina.it

Ivy and magnolia border this grand ceremonial staircase which leads to the Upper Garden of the Villa De Gregorio di Sant'Elia.

Paradise Gained:
An Afterword

The eighteenth-century rite of passage known as the Grand Tour rewarded many wide-eyed travellers with previously unimagined splendours: legendary museums, archaeological sites, noble palaces and a vast array of treasures that were south of Vienna and north of Rome. Travellers whose more erratic itinerary plans took them further south, all the way to southern Italy's Campania region, were fortunate to reap an additional bounty: the historic, extravagantly flowering gardens of Naples, Capri, Ravello, and other towns and villages scattered along the Amalfi coast. By the time my own *petit tour* of this paradisical part of the world – undertaken to gather material for this book – came to a close, I had savoured it all.

The seeds for my Campania odyssey had been planted years before at New York City's Institute of Fine Arts, where I studied the Italian Renaissance during the reign of the late Sir John Pope-Hennessy, a towering potentate in the field of art history. His classes imbued me with an enduring love of fine art and the qualities of beauty found in its myriad manifestations, such as castles, palazzi and villas. Since then, the ports of call in my journeys have come under the heading of 'continuing studies, self-imposed'. One of these trips was to the Roman palazzo of Count and Countess Ferdinand Pecci-Blunt to write it up for *Town & Country* in 1990. But before calling on their sixteenth-century abode, I visited their legendary Villa Marlia (a Lucca estate once owned by Napoleon's sister and alluded to in the very first line of Tolstoy's *War and Peace*). The garden there was the most beautiful thing that had ever appeared in my life.

Until then, my interests were fixed largely on the dazzling interiors of grand Renaissance *saloni*. Suddenly, the transfixing sight of the palazzo's *teatro di verdure* evoked an urge, akin to a *gran passione*, to pursue this 'exterior' form of Italian decoration – *giardini*. Newly inspired, I set myself the task of exploring the Boot, starting at the top, and before long found myself at the foot, and face to face with the prodigally floriferous, preposterously romantic region of the Amalfi coast. There I found, horticulturally speaking, *il paradiso*.

Or, at the very least, I felt I was halfway to heaven. Sitting upon the terrace of the Cappuccini Convento, which clings tenaciously to the Monte Falconetto on a rocky shelf 152 metres/500 feet above the sea, I remembered the maxim: 'For those who live in Amalfi waking up in Paradise will be a day just like any other.' Not everyone is rendered speechless by the view from this belvedere – Longfellow, for one, wrote one of his most famous poems to honour this spot – but most are reduced to stunned silence. Framed by rustling bougainvillea, time-stained pillars and antique pilgrim lanterns is a vista of such light and space that to describe it as a mere landscape seems leaden. Below, far below, is a seamless panorama of Amalfi, shining medievally bright in the sunlight. Immortalized in postcards and paintings, this famed vista became one of the first travel icons of the nineteenth century. After a few minutes on the sun-dappled terrace I understood why this hotel, founded as a Cistercian monastery in the thirteenth century, had become favoured by such *grantouristi* as Wagner (who forsook his room to sleep under the terraces' ambuscades of frangipani). My first impressions were confirmed by the hotel's chatelaine, the Contessa Vallefiorita, an elegant octogenarian grande dame: seeing my reaction to the hotel's sky-kissing perch she smiled and noted, 'One more step higher and . . .'

Ever since that meeting, it has been, indeed, heavenly to be welcomed by many other people whose selfless efforts are responsible for Campania being the Edenic spot it is today. Of the numerous people whose knowledge, generosity and wise counsel led me down many a garden path, leading the list must be Baron Massimo Ricciardi, whose angelic wings, though invisible to ordinary mortals, have held me aloft throughout my journey. One of the foremost botanists in Italy and long-time professor at the Orto Botanico della Facoltà di Agraria dell'Università di Napoli Federico II, he is the author of several definitive books, including *La Flora Illustrata di Capri* (1991) and *La Flora di Campi Flegrei* (2006). I was truly lucky when his professional expertise became personal upon his invitation to call his family's residence my Neapolitan home-away-from-home (now that his three sons have moved out). Looming over the Chiaia district for centuries, its *piano nobile* presided over by Principe

Francesco d'Avalos (one of Italy's most noted composers), the Palazzo d'Avalos became, thanks to its vast park, my oasis of tranquillity in a volcanically noisy city. During the day, *il professore* was an incredible passepartout to people and gardens. During the night, upon truly fortunate occasions, his feasts of scientific knowledge became bona-fide feasts, with perfect risottos served up from eighteenth-century recipes by his lovely wife, Flaminia. Without the baron's palatial welcome mat, scholarly counsel and air-conditioned car this book would never have been published. I should note, however, that because of his work preparing the second edition of his Capri book and the first edition of his *Campi Flegrei* opus, he was not able to check or vet any of my text.

It would not be fair to bring the record of this pilgrimage to a close without acknowledging the role of the owner-curators of the gardens in framing a valuable new truth: that a well-designed and well-tended garden can be as much a work of art as a masterly painting. The diligence with which the Principessa Maria d'Avalos – Massimo's cousin – oversees the splendid gardens of the Villa d'Avalos is matched only by the care exercised by Mariano and Rita Pane at their exquisite Villa Tritone, which in turn is mirrored by the work of Silvana Cuomo – a sister of Signora Pane – at the Villa Silvana in Sorrento. In the category of minor miracles is the story of Giovanni Russo, whose vision and gallant determination transformed the rocky terrain of Li Galli into the enchanted and verdant kingdom on view today. Not far away as the crow flies is another corner of paradise, the island of Capri, where Signor Francesco Ricci has restored writer Graham Greene's Villa Il Rosaio estate to its earlier glory.

Back on the mainland, the same strain of dedication has preserved a host of venerable estates in prime condition, including those of Principe Massimo Lancelotti (Lauro), Contessa Cettina Lanzara (Nocera) and Principessa Uzza de Gregorio di Sant' Elia (Portici). The public is the winner with gardens maintained under professional management, and special thanks are accorded to Alessandra Vinciquerra, the director of La Mortella, and Dr Secondo Amalfitano (and chief assistant, Monia Belloro), director of the Villa Rufolo.

Many alluring choices of hospitable lodgings further bejewelled with radiant *giardini* await travellers seeking a day in the Campania sun. Among standouts on the Amalfi coast is the Hotel Il San Pietro, where Signora Virginia Attanasio Cinque dispenses the same care to a single overnighter as to a rock star or a Rockefeller; a sister, Marilu Attanasio, carries on the same tradition at her family's Hotel Palazzo Murat; Carmella Gambardella presides over the Hotel Santa Caterina, aided by family members, with loving care and devotion; the aura of the Hotel Villa Cimbrone, a Shangri-La set in the most splendid spot in the world and owned and hosted by Signora Paola Vuilleumier and her brother, Giorgio, casts a discreet sparkle over this sisterhood of fine hostelries. To this duo, and all the other owners of gardens in this book, I extend *l'applauso di tutti*.

In addition to these kind owners and administrators, I have received assistance from a wide array of publications. While its gardens have received much less attention than those of northern and central Italy, Campania is far from virgin soil. There are few overviews but M.T. Train's lush *Gardens of Naples* (1995) made this traveller enamoured of the region even before his first visit. For a nearly petal-by-petal analysis of many gardens in and around Naples, garden *appassioniati* will enjoy Patrizia Spinelli Napoletano's *L'Arte dei Giardini nel Tempo* (2000) and *I Giardini Segreti di Napoli: Fuori le Mura* (1996). Campania has long been favoured by foreigners and their travels are superlatively covered in three classics: *Siren Land* by Norman Douglas (1927), *The Masque of Capri* by Edwin Cerio (1957) and *The Story of San Michele* (1929) by Axel Munthe, as well as Dieter Richter's impressive *Viaggiatori Stranieri nel Sud* (1985). For Posillipo, the best books are Valentina Gison's *Posillipo Nell'Ottocento* (1998) and Domencico Viggiani's *I Tempi di Posillipo* (1989). On the Vesuvian villas, check out Celeste Fidora's *Ville de Delizie Vesuviane del '700* (2004). As for studies of individual gardens, the following are most informative: for La Mortella, Lady Susana Walton's *La Mortella: An Italian Garden Paradise* (2002); for Villa San Michele, Levente A.S. Erdeos's *Axel Munthe's Villa in the Capri Sun* (2006) and Bengt Jangfeldt's *Axel Munthe: The Road to San Michele* (2008);

for the Parco dei Principi, Domenico Rea's *Villa Cortchacow* (1988); for the Castello Lancellotti, Pasquale Moschiano's *Castello Lancellotti* (2001); for the Villa Rufolo, Jill Caskey's *Art and Patronage in the Medieval Mediterranean: Merchant Culture in the Region of Amalfi* (2004) and Sir Francis Neville Reid's groundbreaking *Ravello* (ed. E. Allen, 2000); for La Certosella, Villa Il Rosaio and all the magnificent gardens of Edwin Cerio, Gaetana Cantone's *Dolce agli occhi è la Casa di Capri* (2004); for the Villa Cimbrone, Charles Quest-Riston's *The English Garden Abroad* (1996); for the gardens at the Reggia di Portici, Stefano Mazzoleni's *L'Orto Botanico di Portici* (1990); and for Li Galli, Romolo Ercolino's *The Siren Isles 'Li Galli'* (1998). For scholarly spadework, see the ongoing studies of Pasquale Belfiore and Maria Luisa Margiotta, including their contributions to *La Memoria, Il Tempo, La Storia nel Giardino Italiano fra '800 e '900*, edited by Vincenzo Cazzotto (1999) along with the many publications sponsored by *Tra Cattedrali di Roccia* (2004).

I owe the honour of adding an entry to this literature to Frances Lincoln. In my estimation, the bar was set high for garden books in 2001 when Frances Lincoln published Vivian Russell's *Edith Wharton's Italian Gardens*. You can imagine my delight when I learned my title was to be published by the very same house. Immeasurable gratitude is owed to its editorial director, Andrew Dunn – a gentleman I expected, but a maestro? – whose piercing sagacity, brotherly spirit and, above all, patience led to this project's happy ending. Among other wise moves, he intuitively paired *Close to Paradise* with a sympathetic editor and designer team, Anne Askwith and Arianna Osti, respectively, each of whom gave more than their all, if that is possible, to the project. Ms Askwith (who also edited Vivian Russell's title) undertook the at times thankless task of sifting the verbal soil, then deftly and diplomatically pruning away the weedy matter.

My still-evolving itinerary has so far taken me from the revered halls of art to the more lively art of travel, whose snap-crackle-and-pop sideshow is always music to my ears. Halfway into a decade of editorial work at Fodor's Travel Publications, *Escape to the Amalfi Coast*, my first photo-essay book, was published in 1999. In 2002, we expanded this material for the launch of a first edition of *Fodor's Naples, Capri, and the Amalfi Coast* guidebook. Special thanks are due to Linda Cabasin, Fodor's editorial director, for nurturing these and other efforts and for allowing me to complement ephemeral visits to such worlds as those with a narrative echo in print.

On a more personal note, I plan to continue to make payments against the giant, continually growing, debt I owe to three lifelong friends, Perry Janoski, Elissa Rioux and Arlene Wise, whose collective wit, warmth and wisdom comforted and supported me over many a moment when the light appeared to dim. Effusive thanks are also due to Mark Walters and Fiorella Squillante in Naples for assistance and support.

Finally, in lieu of a vanload of 'Gloire Lyonnaise' roses, I present this book to my mother, Rosemary Biery, as a *particolare ringrazia* for all her help and guidance over the years.

Index

Page numbers in *italic* refer to illustrations

PICTURE CREDITS

In La Mortella, a garden where fountains and pools are paramount, aquatic plants and flowers take pride of place, with water lilies — especially blue *Nymphaea caerulea* from the Nile — and *Nelumbo nucifera* lotus flowers featured prominently in such areas as the Crocodile Pool, the Thai Garden and the Victoria House.